1001 Ways to Say Thank You

Gail Hamilton

Hamilton House

National Library of Canada Cataloguing in Publication Data

Hamilton, Gail (Margaret Gail)
 1001ways to say thank you / Gail Hamilton

Previous ed. published under the title Saying thank you
ISBN 978-0-9680853-8-7

 1. Thank-you notes. 2.Letter writing.
3. English language–Terms and phrases.
I. Title. II Title: One thousand one ways to say
thank you

BJ2101.H34 2008   395.4   C2008-901583-5

Hamilton House, 630 County Rd. 14
RR3 Demorestville, ON, K0K 1W0, Canada

Contents

Section One

Section Two

Section Three

Section Four

Section Five

Introduction

You can never express gratitude often enough. Everyone loves to be thanked. And thanking others makes you feel terrific.

A sincerely expressed thanks is a powerful thing. It will bring smiles, bind the heart and sometimes move to tears. In your personal life, you reach out to family and friends to show how much you care. In the world of business, politics or charitable endeavor, it oils the wheels, tells colleagues and contributors they are appreciated and conveys how strongly you recognize the efforts of others.

No matter who you are, at work or at home, you have reason to thank others, every day and often.

You might work with a nonprofit organization and be in charge of thanking donors, sponsors, volunteers, and members who give so generously of their time or their pocketbooks. Whether they contributed extra to help you through a financial crunch, wrote a letter on behalf of an urgent cause or showed up in the rain on Clean Our Park Day, they deserve appreciation. And, of course, the letter is an excellent way to suggest further contributions.

If you are in business, you might want to thank new customers for making their first purchase, thank colleagues or staff for their outstanding effort in the latest sales campaign. You might be looking for a new career and need to thank all those who gave you references, interviews and a boost along the way. You might want to thank a business for excellent service or for responding promptly to your concerns.

Thank you notes for gifts of every sort are *de rigeur*. You also need to thank those who provided hospitality, slipped you a loan when you needed it most, gave a speech at your model railroad club, assisted your aged parents or went door to door to help you get elected. Thank your family for sticking by you through thick and thin no matter what they think privately. And thank your best friend for being such a good friend.

Yet thank you letters, perhaps because emotion is so openly expressed, are difficult for many and are often put off until the last moment or beyond . They arrive late or, out of sheer embarrassment for waiting so long, never get written at all.

The same goes for letters of apology or condolence so necessary in reaching out to those around us.

This book, by putting the language of gratitude, apology and condolence at your fingertips, is meant to ensure that your letters remain not only some of the warmest to write but also some of the easiest.

Writing Your Thank You Letter

A written thank you is always much more impressive than a quick phone call or an ephemeral, hastily dashed off e-mail. It shows you care enough to make the extra effort.

BE PROMPT

Though it is better for your letter to arrive late than never, respond as promptly as you can.

> Write within a day or two for dinner and within two or three days after receiving hospitality.

> You have about two weeks to thank for gifts unless they are wedding gifts, in which case you send notes right after the honeymoon.

> To answer expressions of sympathy for a loss or death, it is fine to reply within six weeks when you a feeling up to the task. In all cases, keep careful track of who did what.

STYLE

Fortunately for all of us, the form of a thank you letter is simple. The style and degree of formality is determined by the party you are addressing. A formal letter strictly observes all the rules of letter writing which can be found in many excellent reference books. A few lines of thanks to a close friend can be dashed off by hand on a leaf of pink bunny note paper.

Simple, clear English conveys the most sincerity. Be direct, brief and to the point. Unless you have reason to expand, it's best to keep to a single page. Take an easy, conversational tone, just as though you are talking face to face. Let your words flow straight from the heart.

START

Always address your letter to a specific person, not a department or a title. When a gift comes from a number of different people, each must receive a thank you note. Begin with the reason you are expressing your appreciation:

>"Thank you so much for the lovely lava lamp you gave me for my birthday."

>"I appreciate the time you took from your busy schedule last week to meet with me yesterday."

>"I don't know what our charity would do without generous donors like you."

MIDDLE

Expand your appreciation by explaining how what you are thanking for made you feel, affected you life or thoroughly delighted you. Recognize thoughtfulness and generosity.

>"The lava lamp is a perfect match for my orange shag rug and fits right in with our retro decor. Every time I turn it on, I will remember your thoughtfulness and be transported back to the that first college dorm we decorated together."

>"The advice and contacts you so kindly provided have already helped enormously in developing the project. Ms. Wilma Haney has agreed to analyse our marketing plan. You have greatly improved our prospects of success."

>"Your donation provided a new water pump for a well in Africa so village children could finally have clean water."

END

Wrap up with more thanks and sign with a flourish.

"Thanks again for giving me a gift that reminds me of so many happy times."

"Once again, please know how deeply I appreciate your efforts to help me with this crucial task."

"On behalf of the children, I thank you from the bottom of my heart for caring enough to help."

Your prompt, warm, well-written thank you letter will succeed in its goal – to make the recipient feel special and appreciated.

Letter of Apology

One of the greatest personals strengths is the ability to say, "I'm sorry". A frank apology when you are in the wrong is one of your most precious tools in maintaining valued relationships.

START

Begin with an apology for the situation or action at fault.

"Please accept my sincere apology for the late delivery of your order."

"I deeply I regret my dog's dreadful misbehavior."

"I'm so sorry for letting you down when you were relying on me to pick up the club speaker from the train."

MIDDLE

Acknowledge the distress or inconvenience the situation may have caused.

"I understand how upset you were when the tent you counted on failed to arrive in time for your camping trip."

"What a shock it must have been to see the damage my Sparky did to your cherished flower beds."

"How frustrated and embarrassed you must have felt at keeping the club members waiting a whole hour before the speaker finally arrived."

END

State what amends you plan to make and finish by repeating your apology.

"To make amends, our store is providing a deluxe model of the tent at no extra charge. I hope you will overlook the error and consider us again when you next need camping equipment."

"Although nothing can bring back this spring's tulips, please allow me to buy replacement bulbs for all the beds along the front of your house. I will make sure Sparky is confined to our yard in future and hope you will eventually pardon us both."

"I have apologized personally to Ms. Arkle, the speaker. I also wish to apologize to all the club members at the next meeting and to offer my services to do meeting setup and clean up for the next three months. Once again, I hope you will forgive my unfortunate mistake."

Your letter of apology will give you the satisfaction of mending fences, smoothing ruffled feelings and restoring damaged relationships to health.

Letter of Condolence

A letter of condolence, best handwritten, needs to be simple, direct and from the heart. The important thing is to let the recipient know you care.

START

First, express your sympathy upon the loss.

"In this time of grief and loss, please know that you have our heartfelt sympathy."

"Please accept our sincere condolences on the death of your dear aunt."

"The news of John's passing came as a shock. My warmest thoughts are with you in your sorrow."

MIDDLE

Provide memories of the deceased and how he or she touched your life.

"Paula was person of inspiration and vision. Her leadership guided us successfully through some very difficult challenges. Her ready laughter lifted all our spirits."

"Your Aunt Lucy was one of the kindest people I have known. She always had a warm hug for every child on the street."

"When I was just starting out, John very kindly sent clients my way. His generosity helped my fledgling business enormously in those lean early days."

END

Offer words of comfort and help.

"I'm sure many wonderful memories will sustain you in the difficult days ahead."

"Take comfort in knowing how deeply she loved you and your family."

"Our family will take over your garden care until you are feeling better."

The warmth of your words will bring solace and support when they are needed most.

Section One

Thank You

ABILITY
- You have a wonderful ability to get things done
- Proud to know someone of your abilities
- You always have the ability to make things better
- Impressed with your abilities from the start
- Ability you have shown in a number of enterprises

See also: GIFT, SKILL, TALENT

ACCOMPLISH
- You accomplished so much under very difficult circumstances
- You have accomplished the impossible
- I only wish everyone could see what has been accomplished
- You really have accomplished something big

Accomplish: perform, do, discharge, execute, carry out, fulfil, realize, manage, bring off, complete, carry through, effect, make happen, arrive at, gain, win

See also: ACHIEVE, GAIN, WIN

ACCOMPLISHMENT
- A magnificent accomplishment
- Exceptional accomplishment, exceptional person
- Take hours to reel off your accomplishments since you joined us
- What an accomplishment
- Taking enormous pride in your accomplishment
- Look forward to your accomplishments in the years ahead

See also: ACHIEVEMENT, ACT, MILESTONE, SUCCESS, TRIUMPH

ACHIEVE
- You have achieved the impossible
- I know how hard you've worked to achieve this
- And you will achieve even more in the future
- No on imagined you could achieve so much

See also: ACCOMPLISH

ACHIEVEMENT
- Many share in this achievement
- A lifetime of achievement
- Even the preparations were a real achievement
- This level of achievement is rarely reached
- We're so proud and happy about your achievement
- Derive great pleasure from your achievements

- You have a good solid record of achievement
- Your achievements quickly came to my attention
- Achievements like this do not occur daily
- Exciting to anticipate your next achievement
- Your achievements in the field are astonishing

See also: **ACCOMPLISHMENT, ACT, SUCCESS, TRIUMPH**

ACKNOWLEDGE

- One of my greatest pleasures is acknowledging your generous support
- I want to acknowledge the kind support of donors like you
- Acknowledging that there is still room for improvement
- We would like to acknowledge the following organizations
- First, I want acknowledge all the effort that went into
- Acknowledge your dedication and commitment in a special way
- Delighted to acknowledge all I owe
- My delay in acknowledging is inexcusable

See also: **APPLAUD, CELEBRATE, COMMEND, CONGRATULATE, COMPLIMENT, CONGRATULATE, HONOR, PRAISE, RECOGNIZE, REJOICE**

ACKNOWLEDGEMENT

- I would like to make the following acknowledgements
- I really appreciate the acknowledgement of such a special occasion
- No acknowledgement can say enough
- You kind acknowledgement meant so very much to me
- Really appreciate your acknowledgement of all the contributions

See also: **COURTESY, RECOGNITION**

ACT

- You've followed some very tough acts
- Thank you for all your acts of kindness, big and small
- You always let me get in on the act
- When you see a need, you always act at once
- With you, caring for others isn't just an act

See also: **ACCOMPLISHMENT, ACTION, DEED**

ACTION

- To everyone who cares enough to take individual and collective action
- Thank you for taking such prompt and effective action
- I always find you where the action is

- Your actions are always prudent and decisive
- Your swift action prevented larger disaster

ADD
- Adds a great deal to our lives
- So happy to finally add you to our party
- It all adds up to pure delight

ADDITION
- An exceptionally fine addition to our staff
- A very valuable addition to our collection
- Thanks for the extremely welcome additional help
- Always you have something in addition to give

See also: EXTRA, GENEROUS, MEMBER

ADMIRE
- I want to tell you how much I admire you
- Someone who we understand and admire
- I admire your perseverance and commitment
- I respect and admire your work
- I've always admired you very much
- Now I no longer have to admire you from afar
- Have found a new reason to admire you

Admire: esteem, respect, revere, venerate, look up to, think the world of, think highly of, approve, honor, extol, laud, praise, applaud, appreciate, enjoy, delight in, idolize, adore

See also:, APPLAUD, ACKNOWLEDGE, APPLAUD, CELEBRATE, COMPLIMENT, CONGRATULATE, HONOR, PRAISE, RECOGNIZE, REJOICE

ADMIRATION
- I give you all my admiration
- Have nothing but the greatest admiration for you
- A splendid object of admiration

ADVICE
- Your wise advice is much appreciated
- You always give such good advice
- Thank you so much for your helpful advice
- How can I thank you for the valuable advice
- Thanks a lot for all your help and advice

See also: EXPERTISE, GUIDANCE, HELP, WISDOM

AFFECT
- Greatly affected by your thoughtful action
- So affected by you kindness I burst into tears right on the spot
- Everyone affected is very grateful to you
- You have affected all of our lives in a positive way

AFFECTION
- Express an affection I have never stopped feeling
- Your warmth and affection make my life so happy
- Always hold you in deepest affection and esteem
- Remember with great affection
- You make me feel surrounded by kindness and affection
- Please accept this small token of my affection
- Your affection is very precious to me
- To remember the moment when affection turned to love

See also: KINDNESS, LOVE, REGARD, WARMTH

AGAIN
- I really hope you can come again soon
- Each time I think of you, I get happy all over again
- Once again you surprised us all
- Again and again you fill us with happiness
- Yet again you've come out a winner

AGREEMENT
- Coming to a very quick agreement
- So glad that you and I are both in agreement
- There can be nothing but agreement about
- Thank you for negotiating this agreement so smoothly and quickly

See also: DECISION, FRIENDSHIP, GOODWILL

AGREE
- Thanks for agreeing to help me out
- A person with whom I can always agree
- We all agree – you're the best
- We all agree that you're number one
- When you agreed, I was dancing with happiness

AGREEABLE
- What an agreeable person you are
- You even disagree in a most agreeable way
- Thanks for making our stay so agreeable

- How agreeable to meet so many fine people at one time
- Thank you for the very agreeable day in your company

Agreeable: pleasing, likeable, charming, amiable, delightful, charming, congenial, to one's liking, to one's taste, pleasant, appealing, attractive
See also: HAPPY, PLEASANT

AMAZE
- You are amazing without even trying
- You never cease to amaze
- Truly amazed at the breadth of your accomplishments
- I want to tell you how utterly amazed I am
- What an amazing person you have become

See also: AWE, MARVEL, MIRACLE, SURPRISE, WONDERFUL

ANSWER
- Thank you for finding the answer
- You have been the answer to our prayers
- You always have the right answer ready
- Our answer to a superhero
- In answer to your efforts on our behalf

See also: RESPOND

APOLOGY
- I thank you for your very welcome apology
- Thanks for your very sincere apology
- Again my thanks and apologies

Apologize: beg pardon, ask pardon, make up, atone, regret, feel sorry, rue, repent, eat humble pie, make amends, hang one's head, lament
See also: FORGIVE, GUILTY

APPLAUD
- I want to applaud your stand
- Every one of us applauds your decision
- A splendid chance to applaud your achievement
- The more we applaud, the more you deserve

See also: ADMIRE, ACKNOWLEDGE, CELEBRATE, COMPLIMENT, CONGRATULATE, HONOR, PRAISE, RECOGNIZE, REJOICE, SALUTE

APPRECIATE
- Truly appreciated by all
- I highly appreciate everything I have received

- To make sure how much we appreciate you
- Your continued support is greatly appreciated
- Appreciate all who have helped and contributed
- I really appreciate the fact that I call on you at any time
- I appreciate your review of my proposal
- To let you know we appreciate all your hard work
- I deeply appreciate your invitation
- I appreciate your taking on the responsibility
- Always remembered, shared and appreciated
- Each of your gestures, no matter how large or small, was deeply appreciated
- It's about appreciating the little things in life
- You'll appreciate the value
- For those who appreciate the best
- You are so appreciated
- To show how much we appreciate your patronage
- We deeply appreciate your business
- We appreciate your business and wish you every happiness
- A way to show just how much we appreciate your business
- The faster your life moves, the more you'll appreciate
- Few things are more appreciated than
- I appreciate you so very, very much
- Appreciate your willingness to take risks
- You'll never know how much I appreciate
- Someone who truly appreciates you
- We appreciate how rare it is to find a real gem like you
- You are appreciated by everyone who meets you
- Just when your thoughts are most appreciated
- I appreciate so many things about you
- Appreciate your willingness to pitch in

See also: ACKNOWLEDGE ADMIRE, APPLAUD, CELEBRATE, HONOR, SALUTE, THANK

APPRECIATION
- To show our appreciation for your patronage
- Accept my sincere appreciation
- Expressing my thanks and appreciation
- With warmest appreciation
- Just a little token of our appreciation
- We just can't show our appreciation enough
- A gesture of appreciation from all of us
- These few words of appreciation hardly seem enough

- How can I ever show my appreciation
- Every year my appreciation of you becomes stronger
- With appreciation from the bottom of our hearts
- I'd like to express our deepest appreciation for
- Can never convey the true depth of our appreciation
- A growing appreciation is developing
- Appreciation changes and increases
- On behalf of our organization, I wish to express our appreciation
- Just one more way to show our appreciation for your business
- There's never a better time to express our appreciation
- In appreciation of our continued association
- Showing a keen appreciation for
- Expressing heartfelt thanks and deep appreciation
- This is the kind of appreciation you get when you come to us for
- Constant appreciation in value is only one benefit of
- I want to show my appreciation for everything you have done
- As guilty as the next person in not expressing my appreciation

Appreciation: recognition, thanks, comprehension, gratitude, thankfulness, thanksgiving, acknowledgement, tribute, praise, applause
See also: GRATITUDE, THANKS, TRIBUTE

ARRIVE
- You've finally arrived
- From the moment you arrived, you were the best
- Now that you've arrived at the very top
- Congratulations on finally arriving
- As soon as we arrived, you took us in hand

See also: COME

ASK
- So very kind of you to ask me
- Thanks for asking
- No matter what we ask, you always come through
- How comforting to know I can always ask this of you
- You helping out without being asked
- I was so glad when you asked
- You did so much more than asked
- Knew I had but to ask for your help

Ask: inquire, query, question, request, appeal, implore, require, invite, entreat, press, call for
See also: QUESTION, REQUEST

ASSET
- You have proved an invaluable asset
- Find you such an asset to the company
- You are our chief human asset
- What an asset you turned out to be
- Our most valuable assets are friends and family

See also: BENEFIT, SKILL, TREASURE

ASSIST
- Thanks so much for assisting us
- You are always so ready assist
- Assisted us at considerable inconvenience to yourself
- The one person who can always be counted upon to assist

See also: HELP, SERVE

ASSISTANCE
- I sincerely appreciate the assistance and support you provided
- I hope you will let me know if I can be of assistance to you in the future
- I want to thank you for your prompt assistance in this matter
- Thank you for your consideration and assistance

See also: GUIDANCE, HELP, SERVICE

ATMOSPHERE
- You helped create a safe, warm, loving atmosphere
- Thanks for providing such a pleasant atmosphere
- The atmosphere always improves when you're around
- The atmosphere is so much better after you made the change

See also: FEELING

ATTENTION
- Appreciate your calling our attention to
- Thank you for turning our attention to this problem
- I appreciated your prompt attention
- Thank you for your attention to my views
- You always command our attention
- Your close attention to this matter ensures success

See also: CARE, CONCERN

ATTITUDE
- Reflected in your positive attitude
- Your lets-do-it-now attitude sure got the job done

- Especially appreciate your cheerful attitude
- Your helpful attitude has made such a difference
- You attitude gave us all confidence

See also: CONFIDENCE, MANNER

AWARD
- Earned every one of your numerous awards
- This award is richly deserved
- So very happy to know you won this award
- Congratulations on winning such a prestigious award
- I share this award with so many
- So impressed with your latest award

See also: ACHIEVEMENT, ACCOMPLISHMENT

AWE
- In awe of all you have accomplished
- We can only stand in awe
- Truly awed by your amazing advance
- Quickly overcome with awe at your achievement

See also: AMAZE, OVERWHELM

BEAUTIFUL
- Beautiful beyond compare
- The most beautiful ones I have ever seen
- Such a beautiful sentiment so beautifully put
- What a beautiful gesture
- Your beautiful gift is gracing our mantelpiece right now

Beautiful: attractive, comely, handsome, glamorous, good-looking, sexy, charming, enthralling, enchanting, alluring, winning, winsome, bewitching, fascinating, seductive, enticing, ravishing, personable, pleasant, lovely, divine, dazzling, radiant, resplendent, matchless, unequalled, shining, pretty

See also: CHARMING

BEAUTY
- Simply overwhelmed by the beauty
- Beauty that takes my breath away
- Easy to become lost in the beauty and the wonder
- Taken aback by the pure beauty
- The beauty of your actions is inexpressible

See also: CHARM

BEGINNING
- This is really only the beginning
- From beginning to end, you were always there
- I want to make the end as pleasant as the beginning
- May this beginning herald even greater things to come
- Congratulations on making a fresh, new beginning

See also: INITIATIVE, LAUNCH

BEHALF
- Blown away by everything said and done on our behalf
- I know I speak on behalf of everyone here when I say
- Appreciate your tremendous hard work on behalf of the company
- Can hardly believe how much you did on our behalf
- On behalf of all of us here, I want to thank you for all your care and hard work

See also: CONCERN, HELP

BELATED
- Please accept my belated congratulations
- Here are my belated best wishes on your big day
- Better belated than never my mother used to say
- Though my good wishes are belated, they are warm and deeply felt

Belated: tardy, overdue, behind time, delayed, postponed, put off, deferred, late, lagging, neglected, slow, last minute

See also: APOLOGY, OVERSIGHT, REGRET, SORRY

BELIEF
- Greatly admire your belief in yourself
- You live your beliefs every day
- You stuck to your beliefs in the face of great opposition
- Your belief never faltered even in the darkest times

See also: COMMITMENT, FAITH

BELIEVE
- I can still hardly believe that you chose me
- You believed in me right from the start
- Proof that the more you believe, the more you achieve
- Always believed you would come out on top
- You made me believe in myself
- You made us all believe we could do it

See also: CONFIDENCE, FAITH

BENEFIT
- We have all benefited so much
- You will reap the benefits for many years to come
- The benefits of this achievement are tremendous
- Extending a thank you benefit
- Many will benefit because you took the time to help

See also: **GAIN, HELP, RETURN, REWARD**

BEST
- Definitely one of the best
- You are the best of the best
- I wish you all the best
- Best wishes for the coming year
- You belong with the best and brightest
- It's great to work with the very best
- Have the best of everything right here
- Always the best at what you do
- You always give your very best
- Borrowing only what is best
- Going on to be the best you can possibly be

Best: unexcelled, unsurpassed, fine, first-class, first-rate, superior, top, paramount, capital, outstanding preeminent, peerless, highest, perfect, superlative, gilt-edged, foremost

BETTER
- Could not have asked for better
- Can there be anyone better than you
- Thanks for making it better
- Become a better person for knowing you
- With you at my side, life just gets better and better

BOND
- I appreciate the bond we share
- Your word has always been your bond
- We bonded the moment we met
- No matter how far away you go, our bonds are unbreakable

See also: **FRIENDSHIP, LOVE**

BONUS
- Please accept this bonus as a sign of our gratitude and appreciation
- You have certainly earned this generous bonus
- And meeting you was a big bonus

- I anyone deserves this bonus, it's you

See also: EXTRA, GIFT, PRESENT, REWARD, TOKEN

BOOST
- Thanks for giving the project such a boost
- You boosted us right out of the hole
- What a boost you provided
- Just the boost we needed

See also: CHEER, ENCOURAGE, ENTHUSIASM, HELP

BOOSTER
- Our town doesn't have a bigger booster than you
- Right from the start, you were an enthusiastic booster
- You're the number one booster on the team
- Such fun to work with real boosters like you

BUSINESS
- I enjoyed doing business with your from start to finish
- Good luck in your business
- Appreciate the generous actions of local businesses during the emergency
- You business is so very important to us
- We have always appreciated doing business with you

See also: PATRONAGE, PURCHASE

BUSY
- Never too busy to say thanks
- I know how busy you are
- The busier you get, the more time you seem to find to help others
- The kindness to take time out of your busy schedule for me

CALL
- We still get calls and letters about how fabulous you always were
- I've received calls all week telling me how beautiful it was
- Above and beyond the call of duty
- We could always call on you for help and advice

See also: COMMUNICATION, CONTACT, TOUCH

CARD
- The arrival of your card meant so much to me
- Your card made me laugh when I was feeling down
- I keep your card on my desk to remind me

- I know this card is a little late, but its wishes are heartfelt

See also: COMMUNICATION, MESSAGE, NOTE

CARE

- We know how much you care
- I'll never forget the compassion and professional care
- People who care are thinking of you today
- I was genuinely touched by how much you care
- Thank you for a day full of warmth and caring
- Please know that we care very much
- Thank you for caring more every day
- The care and concern of friends like you got us through
- Thank you so much for your expression of caring
- Care for it as much as you
- Want to thank you personally for caring
- Thank you for caring enough to help
- Thanks for caring about the outcome
- Thanks for the care package

Care: concern, solicitude, regard, attention, heed, watch over, like, fancy, enjoy, be fond of, prefer, cherish, hold dear, love

See also: ATTENTION, CHERISH, CONCERN, GOODWILL, HELP, LOVE, SYMPATHY

CAREER

- Reached the culmination of a great career
- Your career just keeps skyrocketing
- Your help meant so much to my career path
- My career wouldn't have been the same without your guidance
- A career crammed with accomplishments
- Congratulations on this huge step forward in your career

See also: ACCOMPLISHMENT, ACHIEVEMENT, GOAL

CELEBRATE

- We truly have something to celebrate
- Thinking of you as you celebrate this wonderful occasion
- Now there really is an occasion to celebrate
- Thanks for helping us celebrate
- Come join us in celebrating
- With so much to celebrate
- Look forward to celebrating many more such anniversaries
- Help celebrate a new beginning
- So glad to be celebrating with you

Celebrate: honor, observe, keep, commemorate, solemnize, herald, proclaim, ballyhoo, praise, laud, eulogize, applaud, pay tribute to, extol, compliment, congratulate, hand it to
See also: ACKNOWLEDGE, APPLAUD, APPRECIATE, COMPLIMENT, CONGRATULATE, FLATTER, HONOR, PRAISE, RECOGNIZE, REJOICE

CELEBRATION
- Thank you for this warm and wonderful celebration
- In this time of celebration
- This certainly is a cause for celebration
- We wanted to be part of your celebration
- So grateful you wanted to join our celebration
- We rejoice in celebrating this momentous milestone
- The celebration would have been ho-hum without you

Celebration: feast, event, red-letter day, birthday, anniversary, jubilee, festivity, festival, carnival, party, gala, ball, dance, extravaganza, happening, shindig, wing-ding, bash, merrymaking, folic, jollification, spree, revelry, saturnalia, carousal, Bacchanalia, wassail
See also: HONOR, PARTY

CHALLENGE
- Convinced this is exactly the challenge I am seeking
- This is one challenge you met magnificently
- Thank you for thinking me worthy of this challenge
- Challenge after challenge, you've overcome them all

See also: OBSTACLE, GAIN, GOAL, SUCCESS

CHANCE
- This is your last chance to
- Thanks for taking a chance on us
- Without you, I wouldn't have had a chance to try
- Bless the lucky chance that brought you to us
- Thanks for giving me the chance to show what I can do

See also: OPPORTUNITY, TWIST

CHANGE
- I hope we'll change and grow together for a very long time
- Congratulations on the big change in your life
- You just keep changing for the better
- The seasons change but my love doesn't
- You've brought so many happy changes

- A really exciting change has taken place
- Things certainly changed for the better when you arrived

CHARACTER
- You are a person of outstanding character
- This award is a testament to your strength of character
- You turned out to be quite a character
- Attracting people of excellence and character like you

See also: QUALITY

CHARM
- Drawn to your charm, courage and warmth
- You charmed us right away
- Attribute it all to your irresistible charm
- You entertained us with such charm and grace
- Enchanted by the charm of your home
- Your charm lit up our whole house

See also: AGREEABLE, BEAUTY, WARMTH

CHARMING
- You are the most charming person I know
- Thank you for your charming gesture
- Your charming and delightful solo kept the room spellbound
- No one can do it more charmingly than you

Charming: delightful, delectable, pleasing, appealing, attractive, enjoyable, winning, engaging, agreeable, likable, beautiful, graceful, refined, enticing, alluring, beguiling, diverting, captivating, intriguing, thrilling, bewitching

See also: AGREEABLE, BEAUTIFUL, THRILL, WINNING

CHECK
- Thank you for your generous check
- Your check will make a great contribution to my college fund and my future
- Your check made such a difference to our cause
- I appreciate your promptness in mailing the check

See also: CONTRIBUTION, DONATION, SUPPORT

CHEER
- I want to join your cheering section
- Thanks for cheering us up in a difficult time
- Add my voice to the cheers of praise

- Your cheerful outlook kept us going
- You were the cheer in our festivity
- Our cheers are the loudest
- You cheered me on whenever I got discouraged

Cheer: yell, shout, hurrah, rah, huzzah, applaud, clap, salute, comfort, relief, solace, encouragement, inspiration, reassurance, hearten, gaiety, gladness, joy, jubilation, bliss, felicity, exhilaration, optimism, happiness, elation, rejoicing, fun, festivity, enthusiasm, vigor, frolic, revel, support, boost

See also: BOOST, ENCOURAGE, HELP

CHERISH

- We cherish each and every one of you
- We cherish every precious memory
- Reminded of how intensely we cherish you
- I'll cherish your gift always
- You made me feel so cherished
- So wonderful to know we are cherished so richly
- Always remain a deeply cherished member of our group

See also: CARE, LOVE

CHILDREN

- I wish you could have seen the faces of the children when they received your wonderful gifts
- Your visits always make our children so happy
- Our children regard you as a second mother
- Thank you for taking the children to the zoo for the day
- Thanks for being someone children can look up to

See also: FAMILY

CHOICE

- I think you've made a great choice
- Complimenting you on your excellent choice
- You made the absolutely perfect choice for me
- No one else could have made such a clever choice
- I made the best choice when I chose you

See also: CROSSROADS, DECISION, PATH

CHOOSE

- Thrilled to have been chosen
- We're delighted that you've chosen us
- Just one more way of saying thank you for choosing

- You certainly know how to choose well

See also: SELECT

CLASS
- Everything went with real class and style
- We can always trust you to put on a classy event
- You certainly came through with a class act
- One of those people in a class by yourself
- Go to the head of the class

See also: CHARM, GROUP, STYLE, WAY

COLLEAGUE
- Praise from honored colleagues is the highest praise of all
- You and your colleagues did a wonderful job
- What a wonderful colleague you have been over all these years
- I'm sure all my colleagues join me in congratulating you

See also: MEMBER, PARTICIPANT, STAFF

COLOR
- You passed with flying colors
- When you showed your true colors we knew you would succeed
- Your home is the color of happiness
- You chose the perfect color

See also: CHARACTER, QUALIFY

COME
- You are finally getting what's coming to you
- We're always so happy when you come to visit
- Thank you for coming to my rescue so quickly
- You always come to help when asked

COMFORT
- Your love and support in this recent crisis have been a great comfort to us all
- Just knowing you are there is a comfort
- Have been such a help and comfort to me
- I am so grateful for your comforting words
- You took the time to comfort them in their grief

See also: PLEASURE, RELIEF

COMMAND
- It has been a command performance

- From the first, you command attention
- Your wish is our command
- Honoring you with all the fervor at our command

See also: **LEADERSHIP**

COMMEND

- I warmly commend every one of you
- I commend everyone who contributed
- Thank you for commending me
- To be commended for your courage and sense of duty

See also: **ACKNOWLEDGE, HONOR, RECOGNIZE, RECOMMEND**

COMMENT

- I really appreciated your astute and perceptive comments
- I received so many comments about your performance
- Thank you for your kind, helpful comments about this vital project
- You comments are always the most thoughtful and most valuable

See also: **HELP, NOTE, NOTICE**

COMMITMENT

- Constantly communicated your commitment
- Your personal commitment contributed vastly to our success
- Biggest decision and the biggest commitment we've ever made
- A lasting commitment like yours is very hard to find
- So happy to recognize your commitment

See also: **LOYALTY, PROMISE**

COMMUNICATE

- I enjoy the way we communicate so well
- Easily able to communicate your ideas to others
- I've been charged with communicating our pleasure
- You are always willing to communicate your knowledge

See also: **CALL, SPEAK, TALK, TOUCH, WORD**

COMMUNICATION

- It's extremely important to maintain close communication
- You've taken business communication to a new level
- Made sure communication flows quickly and easily
- Always taken care to keep vital communication lines open

See also: **INFORMATION, MESSAGE, NOTE**

COMMUNITY
- Your commitment to the community is famous
- Privileged to be part of this warm, close-knit community
- We are all part of the same wonderful community
- You've never been to busy to give back to the community
- On behalf of the entire community, I want to convey our thanks
- Your relationship to your community has always been splendid
- You help with so many worthwhile projects in our community
- Recognize your outstanding contributions to our community
- Your efforts to make our community a better place to live
- You have so many great ideas for our community
- You are a great resource to the community
- Touched by the care our community members demonstrated
- Fortunate to have such dedicated people in our community
- Thank you for being partners with our community
- Making the community aware of these generous actions
- Serve our community well in so many ways

See also: GROUP, FAMILY, HOME, PEOPLE

COMPLIMENT
- Thank you for the kind compliment
- My compliments to all of you
- Paying you the highest possible compliment
- So much more than just a simple compliment
- Choosing us was such a compliment
- We have received many compliments throughout the community

See also: ACKNOWLEDGE, APPLAUD, CELEBRATE, CONGRATULATE, FLATTER, HONOR, PRAISE, RECOGNIZE, REJOICE, SALUTE

CONCERN
- Warmed by your concern
- Greatly appreciate your care and concern
- Thank you very much for your concern over our recent misunderstanding
- Felt your concern even though you are miles away
- I want to express my concern
- Reflected in your genuine concern for others
- I thought a long time about how to convey my concern
- Thank you for you attention to my concerns

Concern: be interested in, regard, care, thought, attention, consideration, scrupulousness, meticulousness

See also: ATTENTION, CARE, LOVE, REGARD, SYMPATHY

CONFIDENCE
- Thank you for your confidence in my ability
- I'm grateful for your confidence
- You acted with utter confidence
- Very much appreciate your confidence and interest

See also: ATTITUDE, MANNER

CONFIDENT
- Confident you will overcome this temporary setback
- I was always fully confident you would succeed
- Your confident style boosted the entire atmosphere of our office
- Great to watch you grow more confident each day

CONGRATULATE
- Please stop in so I can congratulate you personally
- I hope you will congratulate one another
- I want to congratulate and thank the committee for
- I congratulate you for passing such a significant milestone
- I look forward to congratulating you in person
- I want to congratulate you on your recent appointment
- Join me in congratulating
- Permit me to congratulate you on
- Rushing to be the very first to congratulate you

Congratulate: rejoice with, wish joy, compliment, felicitate, offer felicitations, many happy returns, bless, hail, salute, applaud, acclaim, cheer, praise, sing the praises of, laud, toast

See also: ACKNOWLEDGE, APPRECIATE, APPLAUD, ENCOURAGE, GRATIFY, HONOR, REJOICE, INSPIRE, RECOGNIZE, WISH

CONGRATULATIONS
- Congratulations to all of you
- I want to begin with congratulations
- Heartiest congratulations
- Major congratulations are in order
- Many congratulations and much happiness
- Congratulations are the order of the day
- Congratulations and many thanks to
- I wanted to send you a personal note of congratulations
- Please accept my love and congratulations

- Congratulations on the wonderful news
- Congratulations and much love
- Congratulations on reaching such a major turning point
- My congratulations and love are with you
- Thank you for your letter of congratulations
- Congratulations on spreading your wings
- Congratulations on opening your own business

See also: **COMPLIMENTS, FELICITATIONS, PRAISE**

CONSIDER
- Thank you for considering the possibility
- Please consider it done
- Thank you for considering our invitation
- So grateful you considered taking me on

See also: **LISTEN, THINK**

CONSIDERATION
- I appreciate your careful consideration
- I know you gave this very serious consideration
- In consideration of all you have contributed
- You always have so much consideration for others

See also: **ATTENTION, CARE, CONCERN, THOUGHTFULNESS**

CONTACT
- We will contact you as soon as possible
- From first contact, you have been invaluable
- Thank you for sharing your excellent personal contacts
- Would never want to be out of contact with you
- The contacts you provided ensured our success

See also: **COMMUNICATE, FRIEND, INFORMATION**

CONTRIBUTE
- Thank you to all who have contributed so much
- How effectively you convinced people to contribute
- Can always count on you to contribute
- You generously contributed the most
- The things you have contributed are all around us

See also: **GIVE**

CONTRIBUTION
- You have made a genuine contribution
- Your contribution will endure

- Your caring, compassionate contribution
- Made an essential contribution to our success
- I wish to acknowledge your selfless contribution
- Recognize your very important contributions
- I hope you know how much your contribution helped
- Made a significant contribution to our fundraising effort
- I would like to thank you for your generous contribution
- You always come through with a splendid contribution
- Your contribution will be remembered for a long, long time
- I want you to know how much I value your contribution
- Wherever you go, you make an important contribution
- To recognize your personal contributions
- Judged on the contribution you have made to our lives
- You've made a genuine contribution
- Enabled us to make a valuable contribution
- Your contributions have been exemplary

See also: DONATION, EFFORT, GIFT, GIVE, HELP, SUPPORT

COOPERATION

- Thanks so much for your prompt cooperation
- Thank you for your cooperation in this matter
- I would particularly like commend your spirit of cooperation
- Grateful for your cooperation and willingness to assist

COULD

- I knew you could
- You did it because you could
- You always imagined you could
- Always believed you could succeed
- In your heart, you believed you could win

COUNT

- I know I can always count on you and I'm so grateful
- I can certainly count on you to help convince others
- I can count on you to take appropriate action
- We've always been able to count on you
- You're a person who really counts

See also: IMPORTANT, MATTER

COURAGE

- I've always admired your courage
- Thank you for facing this challenge with such courage

- You hung in there with courage and determination
- Always admired your inner strength and courage
- With great recognition for your courage
- Salute your great reserves of strength and courage

See also: LEADERSHIP, VISION

COURTESY

- Thank you for your courtesy and interest
- Thank you again for your kindness and courtesy
- Appreciate you unfailing courtesy
- I know it was much more than just a professional courtesy
- Never neglected any matter of courtesy, no matter how small

See also: ACKNOWLEDGEMENT, CARE, KINDNESS, RECOGNIZE

CREATE

- The delightful ambience you helped so much to create
- You created a team that took us to the limit
- Congratulations on creating this magnificent work of art
- This is what you were created for
- You've already created so much good will

CREDENTIALS

- Your credentials are indeed impressive
- Adding one more magnificent achievement to your credentials
- Honored to attract someone with your credentials
- With impeccable credentials and a smile for everyone

See also: ACCOMPLISHMENT, ACHIEVEMENT, ASSET

CREDIT

- You deserve all the credit for
- The credit is all yours
- I wish to give credit to all the generous individuals who donated their time and talents
- So much of the credit belongs to you

See also: HONOR, RESPONSIBILITY

CREW

- The crew here was wonderful
- Love to be on the crew with you
- So glad you're part of our crew
- You've been a great crew

- With a crew like you, how could we miss
- Congratulations from the whole crew

See also: GROUP, TEAM

CROSSROADS
- At a critical crossroads, you always know which way to go
- When we stood at the crossroads, you pointed the way
- Thank you for getting us safely through the crossroads
- You brought us to a crossroads of life

CUSTOMER
- We never forget a customer
- We work hard every day to serve customers like you
- Thank you for becoming a new customer
- I like to welcome each first time customer personally
- You've always been one of our most valued customers
- If only every customer were just like you

DAY
- A day we've marked to celebrate
- Hope you'll be here forever and a day
- You really made my day
- I know this is a really great day
- Congratulations on your special day
- Taking it, one day at a time
- You provided a day I shall never forget
- Today is your own special day
- Wonderful to have a day to honor you
- So happy to share your happiest day
- Even though I don't see you every day
- An unforgettable day for all of us
- I'm counting the days until we meet
- Wishing you a super day and a wonderful year ahead
- Remember this day as one of the most important in your life
- Thanks for brightening the day
- The most spectacular day we have ever experienced
- On this red letter day
- I always knew this day would come
- **See also: ACHIEVEMENT, TIME**

DEAR
- You are very dear to us all

- Success is sweet when so dearly bought
- Want you to know how dear you are
- How very dear of you
- Some people are forever dear to us
- Thanks for being such a dear
- Always hold you dear to our hearts

See also: CHERISH, LOVE, VALUE

DEBT
- Delighted to pay a debt of gratitude
- I am forever in you debt
- This is our biggest debt of all
- A debt of thanks I can never repay
- Consider us deeply in your debt
- The entire community remains in your debt
- I know you modestly dismiss the debt we owe to you

See also: OBLIGATION, OWE

DECISION
- You had a major influence on our decision
- Applaud your decision to
- I know how difficult this decision must have been for you
- You always manage to make the right decision
- You are making the most important decision of your life
- Your input really helped us make a critical decision

See also: CHOICE, CROSSROADS, PATH, SELECT

DEDICATE
- Dedicated to the wonderful people who have shown me so much kindness
- At this time when we rededicate ourselves
- We dedicate this tribute entirely to you
- You are reaping the rewards of the truly dedicated

DEDICATION
- Truly inspired by your energy and dedication
- Your dedication and outstanding accomplishments in the field of
- So impressed with your hard work and dedication
- Proud of your dedication and accomplishment
- I truly appreciate your time and dedication
- Your dedication and excellent qualifications
- Expressed dedication to the many causes publically espoused

See also: **DETERMINATION, LOYALTY**

DEED
- Your kind words and good deeds are precious
- So many caring words and deeds
- Now that the deed is done, congratulations
- Your deeds will be remembered
- The time has come to count up your good deeds
- Too many splendid good deeds to name

See also: **ACCOMPLISHMENT, ACT, ACTION**

DELIGHT
- Always a delight to be with
- I am delighted that your opinion is similar to mine
- I know how delighted you must be
- I wish to convey my utter delight in your success
- The whole family is delighted
- Just being near you fills me with delight
- You brought so much delight into our day
- What a delight to know that
- Your good news filled us with delight
- Much to the delight and excitement of everyone

See also:, **JOY, HAPPINESS, PLEASURE, PRIDE, TRIUMPH**

DELIVER
- You delivered when it really counted
- Always trust you to deliver the goods
- Thank you for delivering the project on time and under budget
- I want to deliver our sincerest felicitations
- It takes a lot to deliver the kind of performance you provided

See also: **CONTRIBUTE, GIVE, PROVIDE**

DESERVE
- No one deserves it more
- You really deserve a really special thank you
- You deserve the best
- You deserve a lot more than
- Nowhere a more deserving recipient
- You deserve a medal
- Congratulations on well deserved recognition
- I can't think of anyone who deserves this position more
- Well deserving of this prestigious recognition

- Deserve a resounding thank you
- Only a small part of what you so richly deserve
- Could anything have been more deserved
- You deserve to have a really terrific day

See also: **EARN, MERIT**

DETAIL
- You made sure every detail was perfect
- No detail was too small for your attention
- Absolutely loved every detail
- You took care of the details beautifully
- Your attention to each detail made the day run smoothly

DETERMINATION
- We are very proud of your determination
- Applaud your determination to stick to your own convictions
- Your strong determination to succeed
- Your determination has been an example to us all

See also: **CHARACTER, COURAGE**

DIFFERENCE
- Your gifts keep on making a difference
- You continue to make a big difference in our lives
- You made a huge difference in the outcome
- You are the difference
- What a difference your participation makes

DIFFERENT
- You are so different from the usual
- Could tell right away you march to a different drummer
- You shows us that there is always a different way to do things
- After you came, things were certainly different
- Right away, I knew you were different

See also: **CHANGE**

DILIGENCE
- Your diligence has inspired us all
- Always worked with diligence and enthusiasm
- Picked out the person with the most diligence
- Your diligence at work kept our department running smoothly

See also: **ATTENTION, CARE, CONCERN, DETERMINATION, WORK**

DISTINGUISH
- Very best wishes for a distinguished, happy and productive term
- You are the most distinguished member of our team
- A privilege to honor such a distinguished personage

See also: IMPORTANT

DONATION
- Thank you for doing stuff like giving donations
- Wish to convey to you our appreciation for your kind donation
- I want to thank those who made a donation or volunteered
- Thank you for your concern and your donation
- We appreciate your donations in support of
- Thanks for your much-needed, in-kind donations
- We are so very pleased to accept your generous donation
- Thank you for your very generous, thoughtful donation

Donation: assistance, support, aid, kindness, generosity, contribution, pledge, investment, resources, sponsorship, present, offering, premium, benefit, bonus, charity, alms, grant, subsidy, allowance, gratuity, largess

See also: BENEFIT, BONUS, CONTRIBUTION, HELP, GIFT, PRESENT

DONOR
- Thank you to the donors whose generosity made it the best it can be
- Thank you to our individual donors
- If it weren't for donors like you, I don't know what the children would do
- I don't how we could continue without donors like you

DOWN
- You certainly didn't let us down
- Let's get right down to the point – you're terrific
- When I was really down, your kindness and your jokes really cheered me up
- When it comes right down to it, you're the best

See also: ENCOURAGE, RELY

DREAM
- Sometimes I think I must be dreaming
- If I'm dreaming, don't wake me up
- A real life moment better than a dream
- Making a lifelong dream come true
- Never in my wildest dreams did I think you could pull this off

- Now we are seeing so many of those hopes and dreams come to fruition
- You've worked very hard to make your dreams come true
- Now you have made your dream a reality
- Thank you for a dream come alive
- The achievement is the fulfilment of a longtime dream
- You dared to dream big

See also: HOPE, VISION

EARN
- You've earned every bit of it
- Rewards you have certainly earned many times over
- Your hard work has certainly earned this award
- Everything you have, you earned with diligence

See also: DESERVE, MERIT

EASY
- You make the hardest tasks look so easy
- It's very easy to say thanks to you
- I know it hasn't been easy
- Sometimes it isn't easy to say how much we care
- I find it delightfully easy to be around you
- Thanks for making it easy
- You never just took on the easy stuff

Easy: comfortable, simple, effortless, easy as pie, piece of cake, a snap, a pushover, breeze, picnic, duck soup, content, easy-going, carefree, casual, informal, casual

See also: COMFORT, HAPPY, KIND, SIMPLE

EFFORT
- Really appreciate the time and effort you put in
- Thanks for your unstinting effort
- I know how much time and effort you invested
- Certainly clear that the effort was worth it
- Nobody puts more effort into things than you do
- The many new, exciting innovations made possible by your efforts and generosity
- Appreciate your dedication to team effort
- All the effort and sacrifice takes on new meaning
- Your fine efforts will be recognized soon
- Please continue your efforts on behalf of the cause
- Very much aware of your efforts

- My appreciation for your effort is enormous
- Thanks again for your efforts
- Want you to know we greatly appreciated your efforts
- We appreciate this gift of time and effort more than you can know
- Thanks for making it possible to join this great effort
- Your efforts are sincerely appreciated by everyone here
- Very grateful for your outstanding efforts
- Thank you for all your efforts on our behalf
- Thank you for your extraordinary efforts
- Want to recognize your exceptional effort and care
- Through your effort, we all a little bit better off
- Gratefully appreciate the effort it took to reach the finish line

See also: HELP, JOB, SERVICE, WORK

ENCOURAGE
- Your gift is helping to encourage an increasing number to
- You encouraged me at a real crossroads in my life
- You have encouraged so many with your kindness, your wisdom and your example
- Just to work with you is to be encouraged
- Deeply encouraged by your determination and success

See also: BOOST, CHEER, HELP

ENCOURAGEMENT
- I appreciate your encouragement
- Couldn't have done it without your encouragement and determination
- Always there with encouragement when it was needed most
- You probably don't realize how much your encouragement means
- Always ready to provide vital encouragement
- Thanks to your support and encouragement
- Thank you for your encouragement, help and advice
- Gratitude for the encouragement given me over the years
- I am particularly grateful for your constant encouragement

Encouragement: heartening, ensuring, cheering, assuring, stimulating, hope, boost, build up, arousing, stirring
See also: HOPE, GUIDANCE, HELP, SUPPORT, VENTURE

END
- I want to end by thanking you once more
- This ending is only a new beginning for you
- True friendship never comes to an end

- Now that we've reached the end of your stay with us
- It's so hard to say goodbye at the end

ENJOY
- We enjoyed ourselves enormously
- I thoroughly enjoyed myself in your company
- Now you can expect to enjoy yourself even more
- Just wanted to say how much I enjoy
- Everyone enjoyed themselves a lot
- I enjoyed every minute
- We enjoyed ourselves immensely last night
- So enjoy your irrepressible humor
- I so enjoyed being part of this adventure
- I thought you might enjoy this
- Just wanted to you know how very much I enjoyed
- I hope you enjoyed it as much as I did

See also: DELIGHT, JOY, LAUGHTER, EXCITE

ENJOYABLE
- As enjoyable as it was instructive
- Being with you is always enjoyable
- Thank you so much for a very enjoyable evening
- I don't think I've read a more enjoyable article than yours

ENJOYMENT
- You greatly increased our enjoyment
- Now it's time for you to have some real enjoyment
- I sincerely hope this gift will add to your enjoyment as you retire
- Your presence added so much to our enjoyment
- The enjoyment you've provided over the years is enormous

See also: DELIGHT, PLEASURE

ENOUGH
- These few lines are hardly enough to tell you
- Just can't thank you enough for all you've done
- Words are not enough
- A person who can't do enough for others
- Just can't get enough of you

ENRICH
- You've enriched our lives
- So enriched by your many kindnesses over the years

- Enriched by your strength, patience wisdom and guidance
- Enriched us in so many ways
- What a wonderful, enriching experience
- Thank you for enriching my life
- You companionship is so enriching

ENTHUSIASM

- I've never seen so much enthusiasm
- Your enthusiasm will ensure your success
- I just had to write to express my enthusiasm for
- Thank you for your enthusiasm and participation
- Thanks to you, I'm simply overcome with enthusiasm
- We share your enthusiasm wholeheartedly
- Your enthusiasm seems to grow every day
- Your unfailing enthusiasm quickly spread to everyone involved
- Look forward with great enthusiasm
- Your enthusiasm for the project never flagged
- Clearly, you have the knowledge and enthusiasm

Enthusiasm: eagerness, ardor, warmth, passion, keenness, zeal, fervor, intensity, spirit, vitality, verve, energy, elation, rapture, exuberance, relish, gusto, optimism, hope
See also: DELIGHT, JOY, REJOICE

ESTEEM

- Know that we hold you in very high esteem
- This gift is a small token of the esteem we hold you in
- Let me address you as an esteemed colleague
- Deeply esteemed by all who know you
- Each day raises you higher in everyone's esteem

Esteem: appreciate, venerate, regard highly, admire, respect, set great store by, look up to, revere, idolize, cherish, hold dear, treasure, make much of, adore, value, treasure, extol, exalt, prize, think a lot of
See also: REGARD, CHERISH, RESPECT, VALUE

EVENING

- Thank you for an unbelievable evening
- Never experienced such a wonderful evening
- Thank everyone for making the evening such a resounding success
- The evening slipped by far too quickly
- An evening we will never forget
- We'll certainly remember such an enjoyable evening

EVENT
- Grateful to everyone who worked on the event
- The event was an outstanding success because of you
- Grateful to see the event unfold so brilliantly
- This event is an opportunity to recognize your generosity
- It was one of the most inspirational events ever
- It was lovely to see both of you at this event
- You guys really made this event
- Went above and beyond to make this event a success
- So many guests said it was the best event they'd ever attended
- Resulted in the most successful event ever
- One of the most successful events we've had in years
- This is a real landmark event
- The event will only be complete if you are there
- No one throws parties or events like you do
- Thanks for helping make the event bigger and better than ever
- Thank you for making this event run so smoothly
- One of those lucky enough to be present at this event
- Your continued interest and participation in this exciting event
- Delighted to hear of the blessed event

Event: affair, occasion, happening, occurrence, feat, act, deed, episode, action, phenomenon, matter
See also: OCCASION, PARTY, PERFORMANCE, PRESENTATION

EVERYTHING
- So thank you so much for everything
- Many thanks for everything you and your staff did
- I just wanted to thank you again for everything
- Everything was excellent
- You do everything so beautifully

EXAMPLE
- An example for us all to follow
- An example of everything that is best
- Thanks for providing such a shining example
- When we need an excellent example, we turn to you

See also: CHARACTER

EXCEL
- You have worked so hard to excel
- No matter what the task, you always manage to excel

- You excelled from the very beginning
- You helped the entire team excel

See also: ACHIEVE, BEST, CHALLENGE, SUCCESS

EXCITE
- I am very excited about being able to thank so many people
- I feel so excited for you
- Meeting you at last was enormously exciting
- I have not felt so excited since
- I've never seen my colleagues so excited

See also: DELIGHT, ENTHUSIASM, JOY

EXPECT
- Over the years we have come to expect great things from you
- We've begun to expect it of you
- Expecting the unexpected keeps us prepared
- Always do something marvellous that no one expects
- Expect we'll be congratulating you again soon in the future

See also: HOPE

EXPECTATION
- All my expectations have been met and more
- Performed beyond all expectations
- Have the very highest expectations for your future
- Please don't limit your expectations
- You surpassed every expectation

See also: FUTURE

EXPERIENCE
- It has been a powerful and positive experience
- I thank you personally for such a supportive and educational experience
- The experience wouldn't have been the same without you
- I know we've experienced difficult times and disappointments
- You always generously share whatever you have learned from your own experience
- Sharing a universally cosmic experience
- So exciting to be part of the experience
- We have shared so many outstanding experiences
- A truly new experience for most of us
- Bringing all this wonderful experience into my life
- A truly moving experience all round

- An experience I will cherish for years to come
- An experience I will never forget
- Thanks for a peak experience
- What a rewarding and enriching experience it has been
- Have deeply enjoyed the experience

EXPERT
- Fortunate to meet such a renowned expert
- Progressed so much under your expert guidance
- Don't need an expert when we have you
- You are expert at making me feel great

See also: **PROFESSIONAL**

EXPERTISE
- You always lend additional insight and expertise
- An enthusiastic audience and very appreciative of your expertise
- We need your expertise
- Your expertise quickly found the solution to a big problem
- The professional expertise required on this crucial project

See also: **GUIDANCE, HELP, LEADERSHIP, WISDOM**

EXPRESS
- Words are not enough to express what I want to say
- It is difficult to adequately express my gratitude
- I wish to express my sincere
- The whole family wants to express our pleasure
- Many ways I could have expressed my thanks
- For a long time, I pondered how to express my feelings
- Simply can't express how highly we regard you
- What better way to express my delight

See also: **COMMUNICATE, SAY, TALK, TELL, WORD**

EXPRESSION
- An expression of my thanks
- The deepest possible expression
- I wanted to give you this as an expression of our high regard
- Please accept this gift as a small expression of our gratitude

EXTRA
- You always gave a little extra
- Right away, you become the one who would go the extra mile
- You throw a lot of extra spice into the mix

- Some people are special but you are extra special
- You added something extra to

See also: BONUS

EXTRAORDINARY
- You are routinely extraordinary
- Extraordinary people do extraordinary things
- Then I was introduced to the most extraordinary person – you
- Then something extraordinary happened

See also: BEAUTIFUL, GOOD, THOROUGH, INDISPENSABLE, QUALITY, SPECIAL, WONDERFUL

FAIL
- Without you, we would have failed
- You never failed to be there when we needed you most
- With you on our team, it was impossible to fail
- We certainly don't intend to fail you now
- You came through when everyone else had failed

See also: APOLOGIZE, GUILTY, REGRET, SORRY

FAITH
- You have restored my faith in humanity
- Your faith in me means so very much
- You always had faith in the outcome
- Thanks for reminding me to have faith
- Thanks for keeping the faith when everyone else gave up

See also: BELIEVE, EXPECT, HOPE

FAMILY
- My family and I will never be able to thank you enough
- My family and I would like to thank you from our hearts
- You made us feel part of the family
- Thank you for being such a wonderful part of the family
- I wish to thank my loving family which has put with so much
- How fortunate to be part of such a warm, caring family
- A family with so much to give
- Looking forward to making you part of our family
- Our thoughts are with you and your family
- Congratulations and love from your family

Family: relatives, relations, kin, parentage, kinsmen
See also: GROUP, PEOPLE, TEAM, MEMBERSHIP

FAN
- You certainly have many fans
- I've been a fan since the start
- Count me as one of your most loyal fans
- Accept this tribute from one of your biggest fans

FANCY
- Really tickled my fancy
- Grandmother took a fancy to you right away
- I don't have a lot of fancy words to say how I feel
- It isn't fancy but it's from the heart

See also: **DELIGHT, LIKE, PLEASURE**

FEEL
- I feel like cheering
- You make me feel like singing
- This small attempt to show how deep is the gratitude I feel
- Trying to say how I feel, deep in my heart
- All of us feel you deserve so much more than this token
- I feel a party coming on
- Haven't always made it clear how strongly we feel
- Thanks for making me feel like princess

FEELING
- My feeling is one of sublime happiness
- My feelings about it amount to a state of euphoria
- I don't want to leave a single caring feeling unsaid
- Considered the best way to express my feelings

FELICITATIONS
- Felicitations on your wedding
- May your life be filled with felicitations
- Lots and lots of felicitations
- Our felicitations know no bounds
- Felicitations are arriving from every direction

See also: **COMPLIMENTS, CONGRATULATIONS, WISH**

FIRST
- I want to be one of the first to say, "I told you so!"
- Always first in my heart
- You were first off the mark in this new venture
- Truly first among equals

- Always the first one we look to

FLATTER
- I am very flattered by your request
- Saying this isn't just idle flattery
- So flattered that you've chosen to join our organization
- Always flattered to have you by my side

FORGET
- Never forget to say a special thanks
- You never forget a birthday or an anniversary.
- One can never forget an outstanding person like you
- Your kindness is something we'll never forget
- To forget you is unforgivable

FORGIVE
- Please forgive me for waiting until the end of the week
- Forgive me for keeping the best till last
- Please forgive the lateness of this message
- I hope you'll forgive me for praising you to the skies

See also: APOLOGY, REGRET, SORRY

FORGOTTEN
- Please don't think that we've forgotten you
- You won't be forgotten
- The competition is forgotten in your dust
- You always saw that no one was forgotten

FORTUNATE
- Fortunate to work with the following people
- So fortunate that you are joining our organization
- Feel very fortunate to know you
- Fortunate to have you with us now
- No one has been more fortunate that us in this matter

Fortunate: lucky, fortuitous, happy, felicitous, favored, blessed, born under a lucky star, thriving, flourishing, auspicious, favorable, ahead of the game, out in front, providential, timely, full of promise, rosy, golden

See also: LUCKY

FRIEND
- I feel privileged to count you as a friend
- You have so many admiring friends

- Never knew anyone who deserved so many good friends more
- Proud to be one of your friends
- Very blessed to count you as a friend
- I now consider you a good friend
- All your friends are there for you
- So lucky to have friends like you
- Counting on you as a friend is so natural
- Wonderful to be with such dear friends again
- Once again reminds me of what a good friend you are
- Not only as a partner but as a friend
- Have known you as a personal friend for years
- We look forward to meeting a dear friend
- You have become such a dear and valued friend
- We were friends long before this situation occurred
- Thanks for being my friend
- Thank you for telling friends about us
- Thanks for being such a friend in our time of need
- Among friends who love you
- You certainly have interesting friends
- My goal is to be as good a friend as you are
- Hope you'll always be my friend
- Thank you for being a great friend and loyal correspondent

Friend: sidekick, companion, alter ego, other self, chum, comrade, confidant, buddy, bosom buddy, soul mate, ally, confederate, helper, team mate, associate, mate, peer, patron, angel, advocate
See also: MEMBER, SUPPORTER, PARTICIPANT, PEOPLE, STAFF, TEAM

FRIENDSHIP
- Our friendship and love are always here for you
- Thinking of our many years of friendship
- Such a comfort to know I have your friendship
- Thanks for your friendship in bad times and good
- I value your friendship
- I'll never forget how you reached out in friendship
- The best gift of all is your friendship
- You friendship is deeply treasured

See also: BOND, LOVE, MEMBERSHIP, SUPPORTER

FUN
- You contribute so much fun along the way
- You really revved up the fun

- I've never had so much fun
- It's such fun just to know you
- The fun always doubles when you're around
- An evening of fun and nostalgia

See also: DELIGHT, ENJOYMENT

FUND

- We depend on you to fund so much of what we do
- Thank you for helping fund this critical research initiative
- The funds you gave will go a long way to support our volunteers
- Your efforts helped push the fund over the top

See also: CONTRIBUTION, DONATION

FUTURE

- Best wishes for a bright and happy future
- I am very excited about the future
- You'll be seeing more of us in the future
- You ensure there's a great future ahead
- Now you can create the kind of future you want for yourself
- Wish you every success in your future activities
- Look forward to sharing a wonderful future
- A future that includes friends like you
- You have a splendid future before you

See also: EXPECTATION

GAIN

- I gained so much valuable experience and insight
- Your arrival here was a huge gain for all of us
- You've only gained in beauty, talent and wisdom
- Our huge gains are all because of your efforts

See also: EXTRA

GENEROSITY

- We're blown away by your generosity
- We can never repay you for such generosity
- Thanks for your amazing generosity
- Your generosity is awesome
- Your generosity springs directly from your heart
- Without your generosity, this joy would not be possible
- Your generosity and self-sacrifice have certainly paid off
- Your generosity is unbounded
- Appreciate your inexhaustible generosity

- All accomplished thanks to your generosity

GENEROUS
- You are much too generous
- You have been so very generous
- Such a joy to be recognized so generously
- One of the most generous people in the city
- Thanks again for all your generous help
- Always so generous with your time and your expertise

Generous: bountiful, magnanimous, benevolent, unselfish, open-handed, kindhearted, public-spirited, unstinting, lavish, obliging, accommodating, abundant, overflowing, ample, plentiful

See also: GOOD, KIND, SYMPATHY

GESTURE
- A simple gesture of thanks
- Please join us in a gesture of appreciation
- What a kind and wonderful gesture
- Appreciate your comforting gesture
- This endearing gesture will be forever remembered

GIFT
- Your gift was very appropriate
- I plan to use your lovely gift to
- Your unexpected gift delighted everyone
- What a terrific idea for a gift
- You picked out my gift all by yourself
- Your clever gift was right on target
- Your thoughtful gift has just arrived today
- Right away, I knew what I was going to do with your gift
- Your gift will help us serve even more children
- Thank you again for your generous gift
- The best gift of all was to learn I was not alone
- I am so grateful that you chose to share your gift with the world
- You give us a gift every day of the year
- The greatest gift you can give
- You spent a great deal of time and care in choosing our gift
- A great comfort knowing the gift has been put to good use
- Your gift fitted perfectly
- Thanks for your very thoughtful gift
- No gift is really ours until we have thanked the giver
- Your generous gift is greatly appreciated

- I really value your gift
- Your gift was the best
- Your gift will grow more precious every year
- Your gift was a memorable keepsake
- Thank you for the utterly gorgeous gift
- Your gift will always remind me of you
- Each time I see your gift, I think of you
- As always, you picked out the perfect gift
- We wish to honour you by offering this gift in your name
- Just a small token gift to thank you for
- Thank you for sending me such a heart-warming gift
- Thank you for the exquisite gift
- Each time I look at your gift, my spirits lift
- I'm so glad you chose the gift you did
- Obvious imaginative gift and intellectual grasp
- Thanks for picking such a helpful gift

Gift: present, favor, endowment, bequest, heritage, bounty, donation, offering, contribution, bonus, prize, award, freebie, premium, boon, honorarium, grant, aid, talent, genius, ability
See also: ABILITY, CONTRIBUTION, DONATION, KINDNESS, GENEROSITY, PRESENT, REWARD, TALENT, TOKEN

GIVE

- I really appreciate everything you've given
- You are someone who gives so much
- Never so delighted to give this award away
- If it were up to me, I'd give you everything
- You give richly of your time, talent and resources
- Thank you for giving us such a terrific treat
- A gift that gives over and over
- You gave me hope and comfort when I needed it the most
- We thank you for the things you gave us
- If giving makes life happy, you must be very happy indeed
- You couldn't have given me anything I wanted more

Give: donate, present, bestow, contribute, hand over, turn over, allot, dispense, assign, supply, dispense, furnish, offer, impart, transfer
See also: CONTRIBUTE, DELIVER

GLAD

- Glad to have you on board
- Just seeing you makes me glad
- Glad of heart and glad of word

- Your news gladdens my heart
- You have always been more than glad to help out
- Glad you managed to head off the disaster in time

See also: CHEER, DELIGHT, HAPPY, PLEASE

GOAL

- Your participation and cooperation helped us achieve our goals
- A time to think of your goals for the years ahead
- You've certainly achieved your goals
- Good luck in your pursuit of this very worthwhile goal
- You have made many sacrifices to achieve your goal
- Always a genuine interest in our goals
- We share a common goal

Goal: purpose, aim, intent, aspiration, ambition, end, object, target, destination, score

See also: ACHIEVEMENT, CHALLENGE, VISION

GOOD

- You make me feel so good
- Had such a good time last night
- Thank you for doing such a good turn
- We never forget a good turn
- Good food and good fellowship
- It feels so good just to know you are there
- It was so good of you to help out
- To recognize all the good you are doing
- I just can't say enough good things about
- You make me feel so good
- Never thought it was possible to feel so good
- Never dreamed how good it would feel

Good: honorable, noble, wholesome, lofty, excellent, top-notch, first-rate, right, correct, proper, fitting, suitable, benevolent, kindhearted, reliable, trustworthy, genuine, delectable, agreeable

See also: EXTRAORDINARY, BEAUTIFUL, GENEROUS, KIND, LOVE, SKILL, THOROUGH, WONDERFUL

GOODWILL

- You've helped create so much goodwill
- The goodwill you bring with you is incalculable
- Your heart is filled with goodwill and kindness
- The whole town is brimming with goodwill toward you

See also: KINDNESS, RESPECT

GRATEFUL
- We're grateful for you every day
- We are particularly grateful because
- I wanted to tell you right away how grateful we are
- So many good things to be grateful for
- Feeling grateful but with no one to thank
- We are so grateful for everything we receive
- I just want to convey to you how very grateful I am
- You were there for me and I'm deeply grateful
- I am eternally grateful for your timely help
- Everything was gratefully received
- Most sincerely grateful to you and your family
- Grateful for all your kind assistance
- We are so grateful to have this opportunity

See also: THANKFUL

GRATIFY
- You cannot imagine how gratified I was
- How gratifying to be able to thank you now
- I hope your every wish is gratified in your new life
- Such a delight to be able to gratify your desire for a new car

GRATITUDE
- This is a small token of our gratitude
- Feel a profound sense of gratitude
- I would like to express my deepest gratitude for
- To each and every member we would like to express our sincere gratitude and understanding
- How can I pack a lifetime of gratitude into a single letter
- Our attitude is one of gratitude
- Gratitude is one of the most beautiful virtues
- Gratitude is the mother of all other virtues
- Gratitude is the greatest form of courtesy
- I want to say everything in the language of gratitude
- We humbly express out gratitude
- Our gratitude knows no bounds
- The heartfelt gratitude of those in need
- With deepest gratitude for all you've done
- Accept our praise, our gratitude and our thanks

Gratitude: thankfulness, appreciation, thanks, thanksgiving, gratefulness, acknowledgement

See also: APPRECIATION, THANKFULNESS, THANKS

GREAT
- We think you are great
- The crowds thought you were great
- Great to know we have such dedicated people in time of need
- It was really great to have you there
- You are one of the great ones

See also: **MARVEL, WONDERFUL**

GROUP
- Your group will be the first one I'll call
- You kept the group together in face of powerful pressure
- You really stand out in a group
- Really glad to have you in our group

See also: **CREW, MEMBERSHIP, PEOPLE, FAMILY**

GUESS
- We could have guessed you'd grow into such a success
- You always keep us guessing
- No longer have to guess how good you are
- Guess who is number one today
- Now we don't have to guess any more

See also: **ASK, REQUEST, QUESTIONNAIRE, QUESTION**

GUEST
- Wish to thank all the guests who helped us celebrate
- As your guests, we were treated like royalty
- A few words from a very grateful guest
- Truly enjoyed having you as our guest
- You were the best guest a family could wish for
- You certainly know how to make a guest feel at home

See also: **HOSPITALITY, STAY, VISIT**

GUIDANCE
- Thank you for your wise guidance and instruction
- You always provide invaluable guidance and inspiration
- Your guidance led to the current successful outcome
- The guidance you provided saved the day

GUILTY
- Guilty of not expressing my appreciation
- When it comes to admiring you, I plead guilty
- Yes, I'm the guilty party; I want to be just like you

- You were never guilty of taking it easy

See also: APOLOGIZE, FAIL, REGRET, SORRY

HABIT
- Appreciate your regular work habits
- You've become a habit now
- Saying thanks to you is getting to be a habit
- Laughing at your jokes has become a habit

See also: EXPECTATION

HALLMARK
- The hallmark of a true artist
- You have all the hallmarks of greatness
- Impressed by the hallmark right away

HAND
- Such a comfort to be in your capable, caring hands
- Hand in hand, we can meet the future
- You have a big hand in our success
- Always ready to reach out a helping hand
- What an honor just to clasp your hand
- Your handshake is your bond

See also: HELP, TOGETHER

HAPPEN
- So many exciting things are happening in our lives
- Terrific things like meeting you don't happen without a reason
- You make good things happen

See also: ACT, EVENT

HAPPINESS
- Honored to have you share in the happiness of this occasion
- May happiness and peace be with you
- Sharing in your happiness
- Take this opportunity to wish you every happiness
- Best wishes for happiness and success to all of you
- Always manage to find happiness in everyday things
- Share in your happiness and wish you the best

See also: DELIGHT, JOY, REJOICE, PLEASURE

HAPPY
- I am so happy for you

- We are so happy you arrived safely
- Happy to be so well matched
- You've made me very happy today
- How proud and happy you must be
- You've made me an extremely happy person
- Couldn't be happier if it had happened to us
- Many happy returns of the day
- May each day be happier than the last
- When we heard, we couldn't have been happier for you

Happy: glad, pleased, delighted, contented, gratified, elated, well-pleased, thrilled, tickled pink, pleased as punch, chuffed, euphoric, on cloud nine, starry-eyed, floating on air

See also: DELIGHT, GLAD, JOY, PLEASURE, PRIDE, RAVE, TRIUMPH

HEALTH
- Wishing you continued health, happiness and success
- May you always know health and happiness
- Let us now drink to your health

HEAR
- I look forward to hearing from you at your earliest convenience
- So happy to hear from you
- Wonderful to hear about your latest success
- Don't believe everything you hear
- Did us such good to hear from you
- I hear amazing things about you
- I'm delighted, though not surprised, to hear
- So encouraging to hear from you again

See also: COMMUNICATE, STORY

HEART
- You will always have a special place in my heart
- My heart prompts me to add these special words
- You are ever in our hearts
- The key is in our hearts
- You touched our hearts in a very special way
- May you soon have all your heart's desires
- A helping hand and a willing heart
- Thank you for making our hearts so much lighter
- You always share right from the heart
- You are constantly in our hearts and minds

- Thank you from the bottom of my heart
- Your beauty and enthusiasm will always live in our hearts
- Did our hearts good to
- The warm dictates of the heart
- You always make my heart beat faster

Heart: soul, spirit, inner feelings, emotion, sensibility, passion, sympathy, courage, bravery, valor, stout-heartedness, kindness, good-heartedness
See also: GOOD, LOVE, SOUL, SPIRIT, UNDERSTANDING

HELP

- I don't know what I would have done without your help
- You help far surpassed anything I could have hoped for
- You've been a big help to the whole family
- You've given so much generous help
- You really helped us through
- Let me know if there's anything more I can do to help
- Please tell us if there is something we can do to help
- Want to help you through this difficult time
- Offer whatever help will be of value to you
- If I may help you in some way
- Always willing to help
- Thank you for your help
- Is there anything we can do to help or ease the burden
- You are a very special help to us
- Thank you again for your help and support
- I want to thank you again for all your kindness and help
- You help us a lot
- You are the one person we can always turn to for caring help
- Always more than willing to help us out
- You really went all out to help
- It goes without saying it was great of you to help
- You are always eager to help
- With thanks for your anticipated help
- Your help was so valuable

Help: aid, assist, accommodate, oblige, befriend, contribute, pitch in, chip in, lend a hand, do your part, boost, cooperate, conspire, join in, endorse, uphold, support, go to bat for, facilitate, expedite, bolster, benefit, good turn, helping hand, backing, kindness, sponsorship, patronage, effort
See also: ASSIST, BENEFIT, CARE, OBLIGE, SUPPORT

HELPFUL

- You were so very helpful every day
- I couldn't ask for a more helpful assistant
- I was immediately directed to the most helpful person – you
- Thanks for the helpful hints which gave me such a head start

HIGHLIGHT

- Take too long even to hit the highlights of your career
- Meeting you counts as one of the highlights of my life
- Among the many highlights of the evening, you were the greatest
- The person we most want to highlight right now

See also: ACCOMPLISHMENT ACHIEVEMENT, PRAISE

HIRE

- We wouldn't consider hiring anyone else
- The lucky day when we hired you
- Thank you for having enough faith to hire me
- So grateful to be hired by this stellar company

HOLIDAY

- Thank you one and all for making our holiday enjoyable
- What a joy to be able to celebrate the holidays with you
- Just seeing you turns an ordinary day into a holiday

See also: REST, STAY

HOME

- Made us feel right at home immediately
- You welcomed us into your home with so much graciousness
- We felt your home was our home during the duration of our stay
- Thanks for taking us into your home and caring for us so kindly
- Home is wherever you are
- You have always been the heart of our happy home

HONEST

- Thank you for being straightforward and honest with me
- Thank you for the really honest feedback
- Honest, you're tops in every way
- If ever praise was honest and well deserved

See also: GOOD, TRUE

HONESTY

- Your honesty and perseverance has been most refreshing

- I appreciate your openness and honesty
- Have always looked to your for honesty and clarity
- Your unfailing honesty contributes so much to the process

HONOR
- I cannot tell you how pleased and honored I am
- I can't think of anyone more deserving of this honor
- I can think of no better way to honor you
- An honor you richly deserve
- So pleased and honored you could join us
- Great to know there are still honorable, honest people in the world
- So honoured to accept
- We are giving your gift the place of honor

See also: ACKNOWLEDGE, APPLAUD, COMPLIMENT, CONGRATULATE, PRIVILEGE, PRAISE, RECOGNIZE, REJOICE

HOOK
- I have been hooked ever since
- I fell for you, hook, line and sinker
- You quickly got us both hooked on live theatre
- What a lucky day when we hooked up together
- Thanks for getting us off the hook so neatly

HOPE
- Turned out even better than we could have hoped
- With high hopes and a fresh start
- A time when hopes rise for peace and understanding
- Thank you to everyone who urged me not to give up hope
- I only hope I can repay you some day
- Your smiling face always reminded me to hope

See also: ENCOURAGE, INSPIRE, WANT, WISH

HOSPITABLE
- It was very hospitable to take us in on such short notice
- So exceedingly hospitable of you
- A more hospitable person I have yet to meet
- Your home was welcoming and hospitable

HOSPITALITY
- Appreciate your hospitality more than I can say
- I think of your hospitality with pleasure and appreciation

- Thank you for your gracious hospitality
- You give new meaning to the word "hospitality"
- Thank you for your hospitality during my visit
- The hospitality shown to us was superb

Hospitality: friendliness, congeniality, neighborliness, geniality, kindness, benevolence, welcome
See also: GUEST, LUNCH, STAY, WELCOME

HOST

- Thank you for hosting such a marvellous educational experience
- Never met a more thoughtful host than you
- You are the best host ever
- The best part of the visit was our host

See also: GUEST, HOME, HOSPITALITY

HOUSE

- From our house to yours
- May this house warming gift foster happiness in your new home
- Thank you for opening your house to us
- So grateful we were able to have the shower at your house

See also: GUEST, HOSPITALITY, STAY, WELCOME

HUG

- Give everyone a hug from us and have a great time
- Consider this a hug
- Right away, I just wanted to hug you for you thoughtfulness
- On days when you really need a hug
- Hearing from you is as good as a hug
- Come and get a hug

See also: LOVE, AFFECTION, FRIEND, CARE

IDEA

- I always look forward to hearing your ideas
- Thank you for coming and sharing your ideas
- Your hard work and creative ideas have already helped improve
- Your ideas are always so creative
- Hiring you was the best idea yet

See also: INNOVATION, ISSUE, MATTER, ORIGINAL

IDEAL

- You compromised no ideal
- Always stuck to your ideals

- We always dream of finding the ideal candidate
- If I were looking for an ideal companion, I'd choose you again

See also: PERFECT, VALUE

IMPACT
- Do you realize what an impact you have made
- No one has had a more profound impact than you
- You've made an incredible impact on my life
- Just beginning to understand the impact of your contribution
- The powerful impact of your innovations will continue

See also: INSPIRATION

IMPORTANT
- You are very important to others
- I want stress once again how important this occasion is
- In the midst of such an important celebration, I want to point out
- You made me feel valued and important
- Friends and colleagues like you are so important
- For the most important person in my life

Important: significant, of great consequence, critical, valuable, essential, substantial, inestimable, impressive, influential, highly regarded, invaluable, superior

See also: EXTRAORDINARY, INDISPENSABLE, QUALITY, WONDERFUL

IMPRESS
- I was impressed with your generosity
- I particularly wanted you to know how much I am impressed
- So impressed with how you are able to balance both sides
- Impressed by your clear and reasoned arguments
- All were impressed by your artistry

INCLUDE
- I was so delighted to be included
- Thank you for including me so often
- You make an effort to include everyone
- You went out of your way to make us feel included

See also: SHARE

INDISPENSABLE
- Your help has been indispensable to our work
- You are the one indispensable member of our team

- What would we do without you – you are indispensable
- Very quickly, you became indispensable

INDIVIDUAL
- One of those truly gracious individuals
- The individual attention you took the time to provide
- Recognizing those individuals who gave so unstintingly of themselves and their resources
- Every once in a while, an outstanding individual appears

See also: **PERSON**

INFORMATION
- Happy to provide any additional information
- Everyone enjoyed hearing the information you had at your fingertips
- Thanks for the valuable information that ensured our success
- We had such a great time trading information
- Thank you for making such crucial information available

INITIATIVE
- Thank you for taking the initiative
- Seldom have I seen such daring personal initiative
- You get all the credit for taking such a bold initiative
- Those early initiatives are now paying off with benefits for all

INNOVATION
- Thanks to innovations you have introduced over the years
- Always keeping us in the forefront of innovation
- You were the first to appreciate the importance of this innovation
- Benefited so much from your brilliant innovations
- Your innovations put us all way ahead

See also: **BEGINNING, INSPIRE, INITIATIVE, IDEA**

INSIGHT
- Your insights were particularly realistic, helpful and encouraging
- A person with special insight into the heart
- Thanks for the insight to understand what was so desperately needed
- Always looked to you for that flash of insight
- Your knowledge and insight saved the day once again

See also: **LEADERSHIP, UNDERSTANDING, WISDOM**

INSPIRATION
- You have always been an encouragement and an inspiration

- You are an inspiration to us all
- What inspiration you brought to
- You have been such an inspiration to me
- The source of my inspiration is right here
- Have always looked to you for boldness and inspiration

INSPIRE
- Your choice was absolutely inspired
- You are so inspiring to be around
- It's inspiring to see so many new faces this year
- You inspired me to achieve even more
- I felt inspired after we met
- You inspire amazing love and devotion
- Your inspired idea was an enormous contribution
- Soon invite you back to inspire us again

See also: ENCOURAGE

INTEREST
- Just thought you'd be interested in this
- You always have our interests at heart
- We appreciate your interest in this vital matter
- Thank you for your interest and response
- Thank you for your continued interest and support
- I have followed your progress with great interest
- Persuade you to continue your interest
- Thank you for your kind interest
- Thank you for your ongoing interest in our products
- Thank you for your interest in staying updated
- Excited by your interest in
- I know you are particularly interested in
- I would like to take a moment to confirm my strong interest in
- Thank you for the keen interest you showed in all of us
- Never putting your own interests ahead of others
- So glad we share similar interests

Interest: attention, attentiveness, concern, regard, consideration, scrutiny, interestedness, partiality, preference
See also: ATTENTION, CARE, CONCERN, REGARD

INTERVIEW
- Thank you for such an exhilarating interview
- Thanks for taking the time to interview me
- I greatly enjoyed my recent interview with you

- The excellent interview left me feeling energized and eager to start

See also: **MEET**

INVITATION
- Extend a special invitation to be our honored guest
- Deeply appreciate your invitation to this important family event
- I want to tell you how delighted I was to receive your invitation
- I really look forward to returning the invitation
- Your invitation meant a great deal to me

See also: **GUEST, HOME, HOSPITALITY, WELCOME**

INVITE
- Thanks for inviting me to celebrate such a wonderful occasion
- Cordially invited to our grand opening
- Thank you so much for inviting us
- I looked forward eagerly to inviting you
- I invite everyone to show their appreciation now

Invite: ask, request, call, summon, beckon, call upon, attract, promote, foster, attract

See also: **ASK, INCLUDE, REQUEST**

ISSUE
- Thank you for your work on this important issue
- You always know which issues were the major ones
- Appreciate your leadership in helping to resolve these issues
- Understood how to deal with even the most difficult issues

See also: **CONCERN, IDEA, MATTER**

JOB
- Thank you for the super job you did
- You did a great job in very trying circumstances
- You did one hell of a terrific job
- A very superb job in every way
- Please accept my congratulations on a job well done
- The job you did for us was truly amazing
- A great pleasure to work with you on this recent job
- Thank you for doing such a wonderful job so quickly
- We felt you did a splendid job right from the start
- You really did a great job on short notice
- You do a wonderful job every time you volunteer
- When we want to job done, we always call on you
- Each of you did an outstanding job

- Appreciate the excellent job you are doing
- Your presence makes our job easier
- I think you have done a superb job
- My compliments on a job well done
- Dedicated and proficient in your job duties
- It was a pleasure to discuss the job with you
- For taking on a difficult and demanding job
- Helped a lot of people do their jobs well

See also: **EFFORT, HELP, SERVICE, WORK**

JOIN
- It was a great pleasure to join you
- Thanks for letting me join in
- Joining in the chorus of praise for you
- You joined us on a real voyage of discovery
- Thank you for joining our team
- Joins me in sending you warm wishes

See also: **INVITE, PARTICIPATE**

JOURNEY
- It has been a journey of awe and wonder
- You made the journey seems short and happy
- The great joy of taking this journey through life together

See also: **HOSPITALITY**

JOY
- What a joy it was to receive
- Will add a great deal of joy to our home
- It is a joy to know what a wonderful person you've become
- I wish you joy – and more joy
- You are someone who brings joy into my life
- I remember with joy the time when
- Even though we cannot be present to share in the joy
- Thanks for bringing laughter and joy
- I couldn't stop the tears of joy
- My heart is filled with joy
- Wishing you all possible joy and happiness
- Bring you years of joy and contentment

See also; **DELIGHT, ENJOY, HAPPY**

KIND
- You have been so kind

- You are one of a kind
- Always there with a kind word and a helping hand
- Thank you very kindly
- Thank you again for being so kind
- Deeply appreciate your kind interest
- It was extremely kind of you

See also: GENEROUS, WARMTH

KINDNESS
- Grateful for your past kindnesses
- Thank you very much for your kindness
- Your kindness and good ideas will be sorely missed
- Your many kindnesses will be remembered
- How can anyone forget such kindness
- Your unfailing kindness helped me through
- Sincere thanks for your unstinting kindness
- Thank you for you kindness, gentleness and encouragement
- How deeply I appreciated you kindness and your help
- The kindness and generosity you showed to all of us
- Want to thank you for the many kindnesses you've shown

See also: CARE, CONCERN, GOOD, LOVE, THOUGHTFULNESS, WARMTH

KNOW
- How did you know we needed one
- I'll let you know the outcome
- I know how inconvenient it was
- Extremely kind of you to let me know about
- Thanks for wanting to know something about this
- I know how much planning went into making this day a success
- Wanted you to know you are always in our thoughts
- Please let me know if you can use some help
- We feel as though we know you personally
- Although I do not know you well
- You will be so pleased to know
- I don't know how you do it
- I feel like I know you already
- Share the privilege of knowing and working with you
- We have the pleasure to know
- Couldn't wait to let you know
- Always know the right thing to do

See also: UNDERSTAND, WISDOM

LAUGHTER
- Best wishes for peace and laughter
- You always bring joy and laughter with you
- Thank you so much for all the laughter over the years
- Your laughter warms our hearts
- Your ready laughter has really brightened the place

See also: ENJOYABLE, FUN, HAPPY, PLEASURE

LAUNCH
- Thanks for helping me launch my career
- A spectacular launch to this new business, thanks to you
- What a splendid time to launch a new relationship
- Thanks for getting us well and truly launched

See also: BEGINNING, INNOVATION

LEADERSHIP
- You leadership got us through
- Leadership like yours is very rare
- A shining example of leadership we all look up to
- Inspiring leadership through difficult times
- Under your leadership, we have made great progress

See also: GUIDANCE, INITIATIVE, VISION, WISDOM

LEARN
- I learned a great deal from meeting you
- It was so nice to learn more about you
- You inspired us to want to learn more
- Now I can show others what I learned from you
- I learned so much this weekend

See also: TEACH, UNDERSTAND

LETTER
- I know how hard it was to write that letter
- This is the easiest letter I've ever had to write
- I wanted to write a letter of appreciation
- This letter of thanks is very important to me
- It's not often I get to write a thank you letter for
- Thank you for your recent letter
- Your letter made all the difference
- My first priority was to write this letter of thanks
- You know how much a thank you letter means
- I'm sure you receive letters like this frequently

- I can't tell you how much I appreciated your letter
- You thoughtful letter brightened my day
- Thank you for your letter informing us about this significant development
- Your letter was a great comfort
- So glad you enjoy writing letters
- I just love receiving your letters
- A real treat to receive your letter
- You letter made me so happy

See also: COMMUNICATION, MESSAGE, NOTE

LIFE

- You have a special appreciation of life
- You've made this the most important time in my life
- Have a great life
- Given purpose and direction to their lives
- You've changed our lives forever
- I wanted to tell you how much I liked it
- I know this is a very exciting time in your life
- Knowing you has changed my life
- You've shared some of the happiest moments in my life
- Privileged to mark one of life's most precious moments
- Thank you for letting me be part of your life
- Thank you for bring new life and hope to us all
- We look forward to hearing all about your new life
- The ability to laugh and keep life in perspective
- Convey my gratitude to a mentor who made such an amazing impact on my life
- Filled with dignity and enjoying life to the fullest
- Life is so much easier because of you
- You help us celebrate life
- You are the best part of my life
- You fill our lives with sunshine
- Wishing you all the finest things life has to offer
- Make life pleasant for everyone
- Thanks for saving a life
- You are an active part of effort and our lives
- Turned another page in the Book of Life

LIKE

- You were always liked
- You are greatly liked and respected

- Can't help liking you instantly
- My aim is to be more like you

LIMIT
- The horizon is not the limit
- Accept no limits
- You showed us that limits did not apply
- You never let anyone impose limits on your life

LIMITATION
- You always refused to accept limitations
- You don't know the meaning of the word "limitation"
- No limitations on the praise you deserve
- By gracefully overcoming disastrous limitations

LISTEN
- Thank you for listening
- You are one of the best at listening I know
- You alway take the time to listen and to help
- Just by listening, you changed everything

See also: HEAR, UNDERSTAND

LONG
- It's been much too long since I saw you
- I've been longing to thank you
- Next time, we won't wait so long to congratulate you
- I know this recognition has been a long time coming

See also: TIME, WISH

LOOK
- I look forward so much to working with you again
- Look forward to continuing our dialogue
- Look forward to lots of interesting conversations
- Look forward so much to seeing you soon
- Make us look at life in a totally different way
- We are looking forward to a great victory
- Now you can look back and access your accomplishments
- You made me stop, look and think

LOVE
- Delivered with blessings and love
- We both send our thanks and our love

- Celebrate the love you share in your heart
- I send you my love
- Much love to all my most favorite people
- I love you all
- My love and wisdom always follow you
- Making us feel so loved
- You've always had our love and our pride
- You are a testament to the power of love
- You've always been there to love, guide and protect
- I never knew so many people loved and cared about me
- Thinking of you with love
- You are much loved, appreciated and missed
- Thankful that you always love me

See also: **BOND, CARE, FEELING, FRIENDSHIP, WARMTH**

LOYAL

- Found you loyal, trustworthy and extremely personable
- Well known for your loyal dedication and hard work
- As one of your loyal admirers, I'm privileged to present this award
- Your loyalty has been outstanding

LUCK

- Good luck with your efforts
- Good luck with your campaign
- Luck has nothing to do with it
- The amazing luck of finding you when we needed you most
- The fabulous good luck of meeting you at exactly the right time
- Just my amazing luck

LUCKY

- I count myself lucky to know you
- Know how lucky we are to have you on board
- We are very lucky to have you with us every day
- Meeting you was my lucky day
- I don't have to tell you how lucky you are
- For those lucky enough to be present when

See also: **FORTUNATE**

LUNCH

- Thank you for taking the time to have lunch with me yesterday
- Thank for the time you spent at lunch
- The highlight of lunch was meeting you

- What an enjoyable lunch you provided

See also: MEET

MANAGE
- I don't know how you manage to do it
- You always manage to make me feel wonderful
- If anyone can manage it, you can
- You manage to come through for us every time
- Just couldn't manage without you

See also: ABILITY, ACHIEVE

MANNER
- Your professional manner was noticed by all
- Always done in a considerate manner
- In a manner that made us feel at ease immediately
- Thank you for helping out in such an unobtrusive manner

See also: ATTITUDE, CONFIDENCE

MARVEL
- Truly a marvel
- Can only marvel at your amazing abilities
- You are a marvel at producing
- You turned out to be a real marvel

See also: AMAZE, MIRACLE, WONDERFUL

MATTER
- Letting you know just how much you matter
- We want you to know you really matter
- As a matter of course, you are the leader
- What you think matters a lot

MEAN
- Means such a great deal to me
- I know it will mean a lot to you
- You know I really mean it when I say
- It would mean so much if you would join us for this event

MEET
- I am waiting eagerly to meet you
- Very happy to have met and shared with you
- I look forward to meeting with you back home
- We enjoyed meeting with you about

- I can't wait to meet you
- Thank you for meeting with me so soon
- I can't tell you how delighted I was to meet you
- So glad I finally had the opportunity to meet you
- I've never met anyone like you
- What a pleasure it was to meet you
- Though I have yet to meet you personally
- It seems we met you only yesterday
- Thank you for meeting with us so promptly
- Planning a mutually convenient time to meet
- I am very grateful for our meeting

Meet: encounter, come upon, come into contact, run across, chance upon, bump into, happen upon, welcome, greet, be introduced to, assemble, gather, collect, come together

MEMBER
- Every member is exceptional
- A very responsible member of our community
- All our members were delighted
- So very pleased that you decided to become a member
- Extending a warm welcome to our newest member
- Thanks to all our members for working so hard
- A valued and respected member of our group
- Thank you on behalf of all members

See also: COLLEAGUE, PARTICIPANT

MEMBERSHIP
- On behalf of the membership, I congratulate you on taking office
- One of the biggest membership benefits is getting to know you
- Thank you for helping to increase our membership roster

Membership: body, company, society, club, association, group, fraternity, fellowship, solidarity
See also: GROUP, PEOPLE

MEMORABLE
- You put this wonderfully memorable event together on short notice
- You help us relive a memorable day
- All the more memorable because you were there
- Your gift was such a memorable keepsake
- You provided our most memorable moments
- Sometimes the smallest gestures are the most memorable

MEMORY
- Thank you for sharing the lovely memories
- You have given me a very special memory
- Such a pleasant memory
- A joyful memory shared by all
- So happy to have this for our memories
- Because of you, I have one more fond memory
- Thanks for the memory of this wonderful time
- You have honored a precious memory
- You bring back so many fond memories
- Given us memories we will always cherish
- Thank you for the treasured memories and those yet to come
- Comfort in the many happy memories

Memory: reminder, mind's eye, looking back, recollection, reminiscence, retrospect, memorial, testimonial, keepsake, souvenir
See also: REFRESH, REMEMBER, REMIND

MENTION
- Too numerous to mention
- And, of course, deserving a mention
- Did I mention how much I adore you
- I want to make sure to mention everyone

See also: COMMUNICATE, SAY

MERIT
- Always succeeded on your own merit
- No one merits this award more than you
- You certainly merit a grand celebration
- You've racked up a huge number of merit points

See also: DESERVE, QUALITY, VALUE

MESSAGE
- Thank you for such a powerful and inspirational message
- Your message was so meaningful
- Thank you for your message of appreciation
- Everyone is very interested in your message
- Thanks for taking time to bring us such an important message
- Your message of hope came through clearly

See also: COMMUNICATION, LETTER, NOTE

MILE
- Again, many thanks for going the extra mile

- Constantly willing to go yet one more mile
- Miles ahead of everyone else
- I'd walk much more than a mile to meet you

MILESTONE
- Congratulations on reaching such a milestone
- You've passed a very impressive milestone
- A real milestone in your growth
- A major milestone requires a major celebration
- Together, we've achieved another milestone

See also: ACHIEVEMENT, CROSSROADS

MIND
- You've been on my mind a lot lately
- Thank you for keeping an open mind
- Thanks for keeping me in mind
- Your mind is just full of bright ideas

See also: REMEMBER, THINK

MIRACLE
- You've been working miracles for years
- I just can't get over the miracle that brought us together like this
- If we need a miracle, we just ask you
- It's a miracle
- You've performed miracles

See also: MARVEL, WONDER

MODEST
- You are too modest to admit your accomplishments
- Tonight, we're not going to let you be modest
- Don't try to be modest; we're going to tell all
- You don't have to be modest any more

MOMENT
- Savor the moment
- We know how long you've waited for this moment
- Let us take a few moments to celebrate
- Thanks for sharing such a special moment
- You made my big moment amazing
- Finally, the big moment has arrived

See also: EVENT, OCCASION, TIME

MOVE
- I was so moved I had tears in my eyes
- I've never been so moved before
- Thank you so much for the very moving tribute
- Deeply moved by the thoughtful gesture
- You moved so many hearts with your generosity

See also: FEEL, LOVE, TOUCH

NECESSARY
- Always willing to do whatever was necessary no matter how hard
- More than a little necessary to thank you
- Your smarts are a very necessary part of this operation
- Thanks for taking the time to do everything necessary

NEED
- You were always there whenever I needed you
- Thanks for helping us access our needs
- You filled an enormous need
- You always know just what's needed
- We need you here in so many different ways
- Need you every day, every hour

NEW
- You were never afraid of the new and different
- As new kid on the block, I want to thank all of you for your help
- When we think of new, we think of you
- Meeting you was a whole new experience
- Thanks for bringing so many new ideas

See also: INITIATIVE, INNOVATION

NEWS
- It's no news to us that you achieved such excellence
- Celebrate such sensational news
- I've just heard the great news
- The best news in a long time
- So pleased and excited about your good news
- Pleased to share such marvellous news with you

NICE
- Hope I can do something equally nice for you some day
- You are very, very nice
- Thank you for arranging such a nice surprise

- No one is nicer than you
- You always add such a nice touches

See also: GENEROUS, GOOD, HAPPY, KIND, PLEASURE, THOUGHTFUL

NOTE
- Thank you for the cheerful note
- Your note really made my day
- Thanks again for your note and your interest
- I'm sending you this little note to thank you
- Your personal note made me feel touched and remembered
- Your note really cheered me up
- Your note was a very special reminder of how much you care
- Your note said just what I was feeling
- Just a short note to thank you for
- I really appreciated your note
- A thoughtful note is even better than a gift

See also: COMMUNICATION, LETTER, MESSAGE, NOTICE, NOTIFICATION

NOTICE
- You sure made them sit up and take notice
- It didn't take us long to notice you
- You're on notice, get ready for a party
- We noticed you right away
- Count on you to notice the needs of others

See also: ATTENTION, INTEREST

NOTIFICATION
- Thank you for your prompt notification
- This is more than a simple notification – it's a celebration
- Grateful that your notification came so quickly
- As soon as I received notification, I jumped for joy

See also: COMMUNICATION, INFORMATION, TELL

OBLIGE
- I'm very much obliged to you
- Much obliged
- Deeply obliged for your help
- Thank you for obliging us so generously

See also: ASSIST, HELP

OBSTACLE
- You bravely overcame every obstacle
- You never let any problem become an obstacle to your success
- When the obstacles look insurmountable, you always find a solution
- No obstacle, however frightening, could ever daunt you

See also: CHALLENGE

OCCASION
- I could not let this happy occasion go by without
- On this festive occasion
- Wish I could be there to share the joyful occasion
- How could we let such a significant occasion pass without acknowledgement
- This is one occasion that really means a lot
- One occasion I really look forward to
- An occasion I'll always remember with fondness
- Take pleasure in helping you celebrate this special occasion
- Such joyous occasions require substantial planning
- This occasion is very special to me too
- I know this is a solemn and joyous occasion
- Thanks for making the occasion so meaningful
- Ensure a memorable occasion for everyone
- Thank you for making the occasion so significant
- You made the occasion so much fun
- One of the most memorable occasions in my life
- Hope you will join us for this happy occasion

See also: EVENT

OFFER
- Very gratified by your offer
- Thank you very much for this offer
- I am really excited about this new offering
- Your offer was a life saver
- Acknowledge the unbelievable generosity of your offer

See also: GIVE, PROVIDE

OPPORTUNITY
- Thanks for talking to me about this wonderful opportunity
- Very glad to have the opportunity to
- I welcome the opportunity of continuing our association
- Now so many new opportunities are opening to you
- A rare opportunity to touch hearts

- Thanks for the opportunity to grow in new ways
- I would appreciate the opportunity to serve
- An excellent opportunity to meet
- Saved us from missing this fabulous opportunity
- How gratified to be offered this opportunity
- Thank again for the opportunity to
- Thanks for offering this exciting opportunity
- Thank you for the opportunity to work with you
- Taking this opportunity to express my thanks for all you've done
- Thanks again for an irreplaceable opportunity
- Thank you for creating an additional opportunity
- I really do treasure the opportunity
- Deeply appreciate this very rare opportunity

See also: **CHALLENGE, CHANCE, POSSIBILITY**

OPTIMISTIC
- We're very optimistic about your future
- Your unflaggingly optimistic outlook kept the project going
- Ever optimistic from the very first
- No one could be more optimistic than you

See also: **HOPE**

ORDINARY
- Quite out of the ordinary
- Certainly nothing ordinary about
- An example of how an ordinary person is very extraordinary
- A few ordinary words just can't express
- Saw at once you were no ordinary person

See also: **SIMPLE**

ORGANIZATION
- We wouldn't be the organization we are today without you
- You are a vital organization in our community
- You are a pillar of this organization
- It was a pleasure to learn more about your organization
- You've brought a new degree of organization to our business

See also: **CREW, GROUP, MEMBERSHIP, TEAM**

ORGANIZE
- Thanks again for organizing this year's event
- You are the one who keeps the rest of us organized
- You are the most organized person I know

- The reorganization is a stunning success
- Leave it to you to organize a smash hit

ORGANIZER
- I wish to thank all the organizers
- This could not have taken place without our tireless organizers
- When I heard the organizer was you, I knew it would be a success
- Our hardworking organizers made the event a tremendous hit
See also: HELP, STAFF, WORKER

ORIGINAL
- In so many ways, you are an original
- But the original idea came from you
- Here's to a one-of-a-kind original
- You always have something original to say
See also: INNOVATION, INITIATIVE

OUTDONE
- You've really outdone yourself this time
- Not to be outdone, we are presenting you with this
- You never let yourself be outdone by the competition
- I can't see anyone outdoing you
- You've outdone the previous champion
- I admit it – I've been outdone

OVERWHELM
- Overwhelmed by everything you have done
- So many feelings overwhelm me
- We are overwhelmed with gratitude
- The happiness is overwhelming
See also: ADMIRE, AWE

OWE
- I certainly owe you one
- No way to say how much we owe you
- And we owe it all to you
- We owe you big
- Can never repay everything we owe
- We owe this advantage all to you
- Only a small part of what we really owe you
See also: DEBT, REPAY

PARTICIPANT
- Thanks to all participants
- So many participants deserve so much credit
- Thank you for being one of the participants
- We owe the success to the many participants

See also: **MEMBER, STAFF, VOLUNTEER, WORKER**

PARTICIPATE
- We were so eager to participate
- I would like to thank everyone who participated
- We would like to take this opportunity to thank you for participating
- I just wanted to thank you for letting me participate
- We hope you will continue to participate
- Thank you for participating so wholeheartedly
- I encourage everyone to participate and contribute
- Enabling us to participate more fully

Participate: take part, share in, play a part, join in, enter, engage, contribute, pitch in, help out, lend a hand, cooperate, do one's share, pull one's weight, sit in on

See also: **ACT, HELP, JOIN, SHARE**

PARTICIPATION
- Congratulations on reaching full membership and participation
- Your participation made it all happen
- We count on your participation every year
- Deeply thank you for your vital participation

PARTY
- Come on in and join the party
- What a wonderful party
- I enjoyed every moment of your very lively party
- Thank you for the amazing surprise party you threw for me
- This party is a gathering of friends and family to honor you
- I want to be party to honoring you
- The party wouldn't be complete without you

See also: **CELEBRATION**

PATRONAGE
- Thank you for your patronage
- Your patronage means so much to our business
- So delighted to earn your patronage

See also: **BUSINESS, SUPPORT**

PATH
- What an exciting path you've chosen
- I hope our paths continue to cross
- You always followed the less beaten path
- I wish you well on your new path
- So happy when your path led you to us
- You never deviated from your chosen path

Path: course, route, sphere, round, strategy, track, trail
See also: CHOICE, CROSSROADS, WAY

PAY
- The months of planning and preparation really paid off
- Thank you for paying me the compliment of
- You always pay with a smile
- You have given me far more care and encouragement than I can ever pay back
- Now the big payoff comes

See also: REWARD

PEOPLE
- A great many people have remarked on your skill
- We would like to acknowledge all the people who gave us their love and support
- I wish to extend a very special thank you to people who have gone out of their way to
- It's wonderful to work with such and outstanding group of people
- Strongly committed to serving the people
- You always take care of people first
- If it weren't for people like you, I don't know what I's have done
- Activities impossible without the generous support of good people
- People are still talking about it
- We need and appreciate people with your energy and expertise
- Easily inspire any group of people

People: humanity, human beings, tribe, community, fellowship, membership, constituency, public, kinfolk, kin, folks
See also: DONOR, FAMILY, MEMBERSHIP, SUPPORTER, VOLUNTEER

PERFECT
- Having you this close makes everything perfect
- You proved yourself the perfect companion
- You made the entire event perfect

- Thanks for being just perfect

See also: IDEAL

PERFORMANCE
- Your performance has been unfailingly superior
- Performance is consistently first class
- Thank you for the magnificent performance
- Always delivered a top-level performance

See also: ACT, EVENT, PRESENTATION

PERSON
- Always a take-charge person
- I would like to thank the person but they did not leave their name
- You've made me a better person
- Simply put, you are the best person
- You are a swell person
- You were the right person to ask
- What a remarkable person you are
- You were certainly the perfect person to handle this difficult assignment
- Persons whose accomplishments earn special recognition
- Knew you were just the person we were looking for

See also: INDIVIDUAL

PERSONAL
- I wanted to write to you personally to convey my thanks
- Permit me to extend a personal thanks and welcome
- Thanks for discussing this with me personally
- A very personal thank you
- I so enjoy getting personal mail from you
- How much I personally, and collectively, thank you

PLAN
- I enjoyed everything you planned for me
- Deeply impressed by your ability to plan
- Thanks to your superb planning, we came out way ahead
- I am receiving so much more than I planned

See also: ORGANIZE, VISION

PLEASE
- I am so pleased and grateful
- I was especially pleased at

- Nothing pleases me more than to be able to say thanks
- So glad to hear you're pleased
- I hope this gesture of thanks will please you
- I was extremely pleased to learn
- You've pleased everyone so much
- You know how to please the choosiest people

PLEASURE
- Thank you for bringing such pleasure into our lives
- You are a pleasure to work with
- Take great pleasure in sending our congratulations
- It was such a pleasure to have spoken with you
- Such a pleasure to see you moving up quickly
- Taking much pleasure in your accomplishments
- As always, it is a pleasure dealing with you
- The pleasure is all ours

See also:, DELIGHT, JOY, PLEASE, PRIDE, RAVE, SATISFACTION, TRIUMPH

POSITION
- I am very excited about this position
- Thank you for considering me for this position
- Look forward to discussing this position with you
- Thanks for getting me out of a very difficult position

POSITIVE
- How wonderful to hear something so positive
- Your involvement has been such a positive
- I'm positive you have what it takes
- Your positive attitude has meant to much
- Strikes me as a very positive step

POSSIBILITY
- I look forward to the possibility of working with you
- Your life is just crammed with possibilities
- This possibility really means a lot to me
- You've greatly increased the possibilities

See also: CHANCE, OPPORTUNITY, POTENTIAL

POSSIBLE
- I had no idea so much was possible
- Without your help, the job would have been impossible

- It wouldn't have been possible without you
- You made it all possible
- You showed us how much is really possible

POTENTIAL
- More than justified our trust in your potential
- Gratifying to see so much potential finally realized
- With such a great deal of professional potential
- From the beginning, your potential was awesome

See also: CHANCE, OPPORTUNITY

PRAISE
- Praise from good friends like you is praise indeed
- Certainly I come to praise you
- No praise is too high
- We've come to sing your praises
- You've earned every word of praise in this report

See also: ADMIRE, APPLAUD, ACKNOWLEDGE, APPLAUD, CELEBRATE, COMPLIMENT, CONGRATULATE, HONOR, RECOGNIZE, REJOICE

PRESENCE
- Your presence is an inspiration to us all
- Your presence yesterday meant a great deal to me
- Your presence really made the party swing
- I really want to say this in your presence
- Your presence of mind is amazing in a crunch

PRESENT
- What a lovely present
- Thank you all again for such a fabulous present
- You dream up the most original presents
- When the chips are down, you are always present and accounted for
- So surprised and gratified to be presented with this wonderful award
- So happy to present you with this well-deserved honor
- I was so excited as I opened your dazzling present

See also: GIFT, GIVE, HONOR, TOKEN

PRESENTATION
- The presentation helped the kids feel good about themselves
- Thanks for putting on such a fine presentation on such short notice
- Everyone loved the whole presentation

- Your presentation was both entertaining and informative
- A presentation delivered with the confidence of someone thoroughly familiar with this complex subject
- Your presentation was so enjoyable it seemed to end all too soon

See also: PERFORMANCE, TALK, WORK

PRIDE
- I take great pride in my long association with you
- Your pride in taking such a big, important step
- You can't imagine the pride we feel in you
- You can look back with pride
- Great pride in all that you are and will become
- With great pride we say thank you to
- I was gratified to see the level of personal pride expressed
- So happy to express our pride in you

See also; CONFIDENCE, JOY

PRIVILEGE
- Such a privilege for me to be here
- What a rare privilege
- I can't tell you how privileged you make me feel
- Such an honor and a privilege to shake your hand
- A privilege like this doesn't come every day
- Such a rare and special privilege
- Privileged to know such a special person
- What a privilege to have you grace our home

See also: HONOR

PROCESS
- Turned it into an exciting, creative, fun process
- I eagerly await the next step in the process
- You are not only part of the process, you are part of the solution
- You changed the entire process
- Thank you for facilitating such a delicate process

PROFESSIONAL
- You were very professional and approachable
- We appreciate your unwavering professionalism
- When it was time to call in a professional, you appeared
- Warm, dedicated and entirely professional
- Thanks for a thoroughly professional job

PROGRAM
- Thank you for setting the program in action
- A giant thank you for your generous support of our program
- Your kind donation helps support so many vital programs
- Express my appreciation for the fine program you presented
- I am very impressed with programs currently in place
- Delighted with the facility and the programs you are offering

PROJECT
- Thanks to you, the project was exceptional
- It was such a pleasure working with you on this project
- Undertaking an important national project
- Thank you for sponsoring such a worthwhile project
- I appreciated the chance to look over this project
- This project owes all its success to you

See also: PRESENTATION

PROMISE
- I promise I won't let you down
- You always keep your promises
- Never have I seen so much promise in a young person
- You fulfilled your early promise magnificently
- A person of unusual promise and interest

See also: POTENTIAL, WORD

PROMOTION
- Congratulations on your recent promotion
- I was happy to hear about your promotion
- Your recent promotion was very well deserved
- Your recommendation helped so much in getting my promotion

PROMPT
- Thank you for contacting me so promptly
- Your prompt action saved the day
- You are always prompt and considerate
- I deeply appreciate your prompt attention
- Can always count on your for promptness

PROSPERITY
- Wish you continued success and prosperity
- May your future be filled with happiness and prosperity
- Prosperity is sure to follow quickly

- Thanks to you, our prosperity had increased tenfold

PROUD
- A right to be proud of yourselves
- You have great reason to feel proud
- You must be enormously proud
- I'm very, very proud of you
- We are so proud of you on this red letter day
- I know how proud you must be
- Proud to know such a thoughtful, compassionate person
- I know that you are proud of yourself
- Proud to recognize
- Yet another reason to be especially proud of you

PROVIDE
- Many thanks for taking the time to provide
- Deep gratitude for the friendship you have provided over the years
- You always provided the very best
- Our people are thankful for all the help you have provided

See also: GIVE, CONTRIBUTE

PUBLIC RELATIONS
- Saying thanks is the best public relations booster there is
- Who needs a public relations department when we have you
- You are the finest public relations person we have
- Our public relations have improved tremendously

PURCHASE
- Thank you for your first purchase
- In appreciation for making your purchase at our store
- No money could purchase the recognition you have earned
- We appreciate every purchase, no matter how small

QUALIFY
- So well qualified for this role
- Qualify you very nicely
- Out of the entire group, you are the only one fully qualified for such a tough assignment

See also: DESERVE, MERIT

QUALITY
- Always admire your sterling qualities

- You have all the qualities we need so much
- The qualities you show are simply timeless
- The quality you provided was superb

See also: ABILITY, GOOD, HEART

QUESTIONNAIRE
- Thanks for taking the time to fill out this questionnaire
- Here is a small gift for filling out our questionnaire
- Don't need a questionnaire to find out that you're terrific

QUESTION
- If you have any further questions, do not hesitate to call
- You never questioned my initiatives, no matter how odd
- Right from the beginning, no one questioned your stellar ability

See also: ASK, GUESS, REQUEST

RAVE
- I just want to rave about you
- Everyone is raving about what you accomplished
- There were raves about the
- Your performance produced nothing but raves
- This is one more rave review for you

See also: HONOR, PRAISE, RECOGNIZE

REALITY
- You helped us turn this dream into a reality
- Thank you for stepping forward to make this a reality
- None of this would be a reality without your faith and vision
- One case where the ideal and the reality are the same

REAP
- May you reap the benefits for many years to come
- You are reaping what you have sown, and it's a fabulous crop
- Reaping recognition and awards right and left
- We are all reaping the results of your efforts
- Now it's time to reap your rewards

See also: GAIN, REWARD

RECIPROCATE
- Only hope I can reciprocate some day
- Whatever I can do to reciprocate, you have only to ask
- As a way of reciprocating your many kindnesses

- Let me reciprocate by inviting you to lunch
See also: GIVE, RETURN

RECOGNIZE
- Recognizing those who were generous enough to let me
- Let me be the first to recognize your great achievement
- Recognizing just how much you have helped
- Recognizing your many accomplishments
See also: ADMIRE, APPLAUD, ACKNOWLEDGE, APPLAUD, CELEBRATE, COMPLIMENT, CONGRATULATE, HONOR, PRAISE, REJOICE

RECOMMEND
- I do not hesitate to recommend
- Like to recommend you to all our friends
- I won't hesitate to recommend you
- We will recommend you at every chance
- Thanks for recommending me

RECOMMENDATION
- I would like to thank you for your favourable recommendation
- Pleased to offer this recommendation
- Delighted to give my personal recommendation
- Your careful recommendations proved an enormous help

RECORD
- You are building a fine record of achievement
- So genuine a record of achievement
- We only have to look at your amazing record
- Boasting such an impressive record
See also: MEMORY, REMEMBER, REMIND

REFRESH
- How refreshing to realize there are people like you
- So refreshing to know people who can still think for themselves
- Regarding you, I never have to refresh my memory
- You are such a refreshing change

REGARD
- Always holding you in the highest regard
- First, let me send my regards
- Everyone sends you their warmest regards

- I regard you as a wise and patient mentor
- I can't tell you the awe with which I regard

See also: ADMIRATION, ESTEEM

REJOICE

- Allow us to rejoice with you
- The whole family is rejoicing in your good fortune
- If there was a reason to rejoice
- Let us rejoice together
- Rejoice in the memory

See also: ADMIRE, ACKNOWLEDGE, APPLAUD, CELEBRATE, COMPLIMENT, CONGRATULATE, HONOR, PRAISE, RECOGNIZE

RELATIONSHIP

- I hope we'll always have a close, loving relationship
- Let's make this relationship permanent
- A wonderful sign of a strong relationship
- Always deepening your relationship
- Now that we have such an excellent working relationship

See also: FRIENDSHIP, TEAM, GROUP

RELIEF

- It was such a relief to know you were there to help
- The moment you appeared, I breathed a huge sigh of relief
- What a relief to know you are there as backup

RECOGNITION

- Equal recognition for all involved is well deserved
- It took a lot of time and effort to reach this kind of recognition
- What a perfect recognition of your outstanding contribution
- Won the recognition you so richly deserve
- Recognition and appreciation of your skills just keeps growing
- A lot of recognition is coming your way lately

See also: ATTENTION, AWARD, CELEBRATION, HONOR,

RELY

- Naturally rely on you for help, encouragement and great companionship
- The whole family relies on you for encouragement and good cheer
- Can always rely on you to come through at a pinch
- We rely on you the most for encouragement and support

- Some people you can instantly you rely on

See also: COUNT

REMEMBER
- Helped make it something we'll remember forever
- We will always remember what you have so kindly done
- Thank you for remembering
- You always remember the important things
- Each time I remember, it brings a smile
- I want to say something that will be remembered long after this occasion is over
- You are remembered
- How thoughtful of you to remember in such a special way
- It was so good of you to remember
- I'm touched and very grateful that you remembered
- I'll long remember your kindness
- So considerate of you to remember me
- How did you remember it was my birthday

See also: MEMORY, MEMORABLE

REMIND
- It will always remind me of you
- Each time see this picture, it will remind me of this lovely vacation
- You don't have to remind me about what I owe
- A little something to remind you of your happy time here
- Remind you again of everything we owe to you
- You always reminded me of a young athlete chaffing to start

REPAY
- How can I ever repay you for your many kindnesses
- Just a start in repaying everything I owe you
- None of us can repay you adequately for
- I'd like to repay you by saying
- How can we repay such a compliment

See also: DEBT, OWE

REPAYMENT
- I hope this is a small repayment for your help
- Trying to imagine what I could possibly do in repayment
- Let me assure you, there is absolutely no need for repayment
- No repayment is necessary

REPUTATION
- Your fine reputation has preceded you
- Your reputation just grew another three sizes
- I couldn't believe your reputation but now I know it's true
- Completely overawed by your reputation
- So privilege to meet someone with your stellar reputation

See also: REGARD

REQUEST
- Thank you for your thoughtful request
- When you answered my request, I could hardly believe my luck
- No matter how odd the request, you always managed to fill it
- Express my gratitude for prompt attention to my request

See also: ASK, GUESS, QUESTION, QUESTIONAIRE

RESPECT
- You are one of the most highly respected
- To communicate our great respect for
- Deeply respected, professionally and personally
- Respected as a consummate artist at what he did
- I want you to know how much I respect you
- Won the respect of all who work with you
- Truly earned the respect of everyone in the group
- Always had the respect of your colleagues
- You are a person I respect very much

Respect: esteem, high regard, admiration, veneration, reverence, approval, appreciation, courtesy, civility, good will
See also: ADMIRE, APPRECIATION, ESTEEM, REGARD

RESPOND
- You contribution enables us to respond where the need is greatest
- Thank you for responding so quickly to my request
- Never have to wait for you to respond
- You always respond at once to the call
- Want to respond to you personally

See also: ANSWER

RESPONSE
- I really appreciate your prompt response
- Thank you for your candid response
- Thank you for your compassionate response
- Pleased with your quick response

- Want to thank you for your great response
- I was really touched by the enthusiastic response
- Your fast, on-the-scene response was genuinely appreciated
- The depth of response has been remarkable
- Thank you for your diligent response
- Grateful for your timely response

See also: ANSWER, ATTENTION

RESPONSIBILITY
- One of my primary responsibilities is to thank you warmly
- Must salute the large responsibilities you volunteered to take on
- Taking on new responsibilities for your community
- A time to reflect on our ongoing responsibility
- Demonstrating a strong sense of responsibility
- Carrying off so well the responsibility for such a complex event

RESPONSIBLE
- You are mainly responsible for the enormous success
- Take a bow in the direction of the person most responsible
- How does it feel to be responsible for so much happiness
- When good things happen, you are responsible
- You were always the responsible person

REST
- Pat yourself on the back and take a well-deserved rest
- And the rest is history
- After such a prodigious undertaking, you've earned a rest
- Standing far above the rest of us
- We can rest easy, knowing you're on the job
- What a wonderful rest from my usual duties

See also: HOLIDAY

RETURN
- You expect nothing in return
- Again and again, I return to your achievements
- Many, many happy returns of the day
- What you give out now returns to you many times over

REWARD
- Rich in challenges and rewards
- The rewards have certainly justified the effort
- A thrill to see you rewarded so well

Reward: recompense, payment, return, award, prize, honor, compliment, testimonial, tribute, bonus
See also: BONUS, TRIBUTE

RIGHT
- You were right all along
- You always fight for what you know to be right
- The courage to do right as you see it
- Thanks for standing up for what is right
- Trust you to do the right thing
- We have more rights because of you

RITE
- Congratulations for reaching such a rite of passage
- Solemn rites bringing so much joy
- Celebrating the rite of marriage calls for glad words indeed
- Honored to attend this awesome rite

See also: CELEBRATION, EVENT, OCCASION, TRADITION

ROLE
- You are uniquely suited for the role
- You are such a fine role model
- You took on a mind boggling number of crucial roles
- A role model we look up to every day
- You have played a significant role in shaping
- Certainly earned this recognition for your vital role

RUN
- Thanks for hitting the ground running
- The only person who can run this project successfully is you
- No matter how hard I run, I can never keep up to you
- We always run to you for help

See also: EFFORT, MANAGE, ORGANIZE

SACRIFICE
- Sacrificing your time, effort and money
- With sacrifice far beyond the call of duty
- Your sacrifice had brought great joy to many
- No sacrifice was too great for you
- Humbly acknowledge all the sacrifices you so gladly made

See also: DEBT, GIVE, OWE, REPAY

SALUTE
- You deserve a hearty salute
- I salute your success
- The whole town salutes you
- We are gathered here to salute a favorite daughter

See also: ADMIRE, CELEBRATE, NOTICE

SATISFACTION
- You must feel a tremendous sense of satisfaction
- An amazing feeling of satisfaction and fulfilment
- I get so much satisfaction out of thanking you

See also: JOY, PLEASURE

SATISFACTORY
- Satisfactory in every way
- Thank you for bringing the matter to such a satisfactory conclusion
- Your work has always been much, much more than satisfactory
- Thanks to you, each party arrived at a satisfactory agreement

SAY
- I guess what I'm trying to say is thank you
- What else can I say about such a wonderful person
- Just our way of saying thanks
- Saying thanks is so important to me
- There is so much to say
- There are so many way to say it

See also: EXPRESS, PROMISE, WORD

SEE
- I wish you could see me now
- You always see clearly what is happening
- Thanks for taking the time to see me off at the station
- You saw to it that we had only the best

See also: UNDERSTAND

SELECT
- So proud to have been selected
- You have been selected for this special honor
- When you were selected for this post, you were the right person
- Congratulations on being selected
- You were selected from a very competitive field

See also: CHOOSE, DECISION

SEND-OFF
- Thank you for this wonderful and generous send-off
- We wanted to give you a send-off worthy of you
- I've certainly never had a send-off like this one
- A send-off I'll be talking about for years

SERVE
- Serve the purpose very well
- Very proud of the men and women who serve
- Your contribution helped us serve even more kids in need
- It was such a pleasure to serve you
- You have served us so well for so many years

See also: **CARE, HELP**

SERVICE
- Invaluable and irreplaceable service
- A monument to service
- A free service for you and your family to enjoy
- Savings on service you might need in the future
- Avail yourself of this service
- A low price that still gives you personal service
- We offer services to the general public
- I'm very impressed with the services you offer
- Congratulate you on your many years of outstanding service
- If we can be of any service to you in the future
- Fortunate to have had the services of
- Performed a priceless service
- Like to thank you for your six years of service to our company
- Our appreciation for your loyal service

See also: **EFFORT, HELP, JOB, WORK**

SHARE
- Sharing it with you is one of life's greatest pleasures
- That's one memory we will always share
- It was truly a joy to share
- I can't wait to share this day with you
- I look forward to sharing a very special evening
- It meant a lot to have you share
- You shared a very special moment
- Thank you for sharing your wisdom and experience
- Work becomes a joy when shared by you
- Thank you for taking the time to share

- Share many lifelong interests
- Have a wonderful piece of news to share with everyone

Share: part, allocation, allot, measure out, portion out, split the difference, participate, take part in, have a stake in

See also: CONTRIBUTE, JOIN, PARTICIPATE, TEACH

SHOCK
- What a wonderful shock
- Now that I'm over the shock, I want to thank you
- Shocked to discover how much you have been doing
- Such a shock and a delight to meet you after all these years

See also: OVERWHELM, SURPRISE

SHOP
- Thank you for shopping with us
- I hope you'll shop at our store often in the future
- I stopped shopping for a husband when I met you
- Looking forward to talking shop with you

SHOUT
- You make us want to cheer and shout
- Shout your virtues from the rooftops
- Time to do a little shouting about you
- You sure gave us something to shout about

See also: ADMIRE, CELEBRATE, NOTICE

SIMPLE
- What I have to say is very simple
- You are the best, plain and simple
- A few simple words are hardly enough
- You always made it very simple
- Simple gratitude from deep in my heart
- Your simple kindness is deeply felt

See also: EASY, HONEST, ORDINARY

SITUATION
- Thank you for taking care of an appalling situation
- Lent credibility to a difficult situation
- Only you could have saved the situation the way you did
- You always had the situation under control
- You took a tough situation in hand immediately

SKILL
- You are making the best use possible of your skills
- Glad you can use your talents and skills in your new position
- Thanks for all your organizational skills
- Only your unique skills make all this possible
- Your background and skills make you the best choice

See also: **ABILITY, ACCOMPLISHMENT, TALENT**

SMILE
- There's always room for a smile
- You make me smile just thinking about you
- We really appreciate your friendly smile
- With sleeves rolled up and smiles all around

See also: **HAPPY, JOY, REJOICE**

SOMEBODY
- We have no way to thank that special, anonymous somebody
- You really are somebody
- Appreciation for somebody exceptional
- Could that somebody be you
- You're not just anybody, you're somebody fabulous

See also: **PERSON**

SOUL
- Saying thanks is good for the soul
- Saying thank you really makes me feel good in my soul
- Lifts my soul every time I see it
- You have touched my heart, soul and mind

See also: **HEART, SPIRIT**

SPEAK
- Everyone speaks of you in the highest terms
- Thank you for speaking out so powerfully and effectively
- Thank you for having the courage to speak out publically
- Thanks for daring to speak up in support
- You are speaking our language
- Thank you for taking the time to speak to me
- I appreciate the opportunity to speak with you personally

See also: **EXPRESS, SAY, WORD**

SPECIAL
- You are one of the special few

- So nice to be thought of in a very special way
- Acknowledge a very special relationship
- You are a very special person
- You are very special to us
- Let it be known you are special
- You are part of a very special group
- It really means something special to me
- Love and special strength sustains you
- Reflect on the special times we have spent together

Special: distinctive, singular, individual, one of a kind, unusual, different, uncommon, rare, unique, out-of-the-ordinary, unconventional, novel, peculiar, significant, important, momentous, great, earthshaking, foremost, remarkable, notable, noteworthy, prominent, respected, famed, renowned, celebrated, illustrious, outstanding, extraordinary, exceptional, incredible, unbelievable, peerless, unequalled, impressive, breath-taking, super, superb, wonderful, out of sight
See also: AMAZE, WONDERFUL

SPIRIT
- How comforting to know you are always with us in spirit
- Your actions spring straight from the spirit
- The generous spirit inside you shines out for all to see
- Always admire your strong and soaring spirit
- Thanks to all of you for your kind hearts and thoughtful spirits
- This experience has enriched my spirit

See also: HEART, INSPIRATION, SOUL

SPONSOR
- And now a word about our sponsor
- Please visit our sponsors
- I am very honored to sponsor
- I couldn't have handpicked a better sponsor
- A huge thank you to our loyal sponsors
- Thanks to our conference sponsors
- We'd like to thank our sponsors for their generosity
- Thank you for being our sponsor

See also: CONTRIBUTION

STAFF
- Please convey our admiration to the entire staff
- I would like to take this opportunity to commend your staff
- I want to compliment your staff for their superb effort

- Please pass on our thanks to all your friendly staff
- Thank you and your staff for working so hard
- The efficiency with which your staff worked was truly memorable
- Your staff was very professional and friendly
- Your cheerful, efficient staff contributed so much
- Comforted by the efforts of your staff
- A terrific addition to our staff
- I would like to express my appreciation for the kindness and consideration of your staff
- Your contribution helps us work toward increasing our staff

See also: **CREW, GROUP, MEMBERSHIP, PEOPLE, SUPPORTERS, WORKER**

STAND
- I urge you to stand firm
- Thank you for standing beside us on this important issue
- You took a firm stand and stuck to it
- Thanks for standing up and being counted
- Even though your stand was unpopular, it was right

STANDARD
- Helping us meet the highest standards
- Never once did you compromise your standards
- Now everyone must measure up to the standard you have set
- I know it's not standard procedure to thank individuals
- Just like to record my thanks for the excellent standard shown

See also: **IDEAL, VALUE**

STAY
- So glad you chose to stay
- Your excellent hospitality made our stay very pleasant
- If you are ever in our area, please feel welcome to stay with us
- Thank you so much for our wonderful stay
- Thanks so much for making our stay such an agreeable one
- We thoroughly enjoyed our stay
- Thank you for the kindness extended to me during my recent stay
- One more time, I thank you for our lovely stay
- Thank you for the absolutely perfect stay

See also: **GUEST, HOSPITALITY, VISIT**

STEP
- Want to help you to take the next step

- Watched you ever since your first baby steps
- This achievement is a giant step forward for you
- Step by step, you'll get to the top
- Thank you for making possible another step forward

STORY
- We have many delightful stories to tell
- Your success is a story in itself
- We would love to hear all your stories
- Yours has always been a story of dedication

STRANGER
- I never felt less a stranger
- Your kindness to a stranger is deeply appreciated
- Please don't be a stranger
- You'll never be a stranger to us

STYLE
- Thank you for doing it with such flare and style
- Your style is unmistakable
- Your brought a desperately needed change of style and direction
- You showed us a thing or two about style

See also: BEAUTY, CHARM, STYLE

SUCCESS
- You contributed a great deal to our success
- You have made this project such a big success
- You played a big part in making this a success
- Your help ultimately resulted in success
- Thanks to everyone who helped make the weekend such a great success
- You have a secret formula for success
- I'm crowing about your level of success
- I have every confidence in your ongoing success
- You made the event an outstanding success
- Thanks for everything you did to make this such a resounding success
- Such a great success is achieved by hard work
- We were so excited to learn of the success of the auction
- Have contributed so much to our collective success and mutual prosperity
- Sincere wishes for continued success

- So delighted with your recent success
- The success is due in no small way to your support and advocacy

See also: ACCOMPLISHMENT, ACHIEVEMENT

SUGGESTION
- Always open to suggestions
- Your ideas and suggestions are greatly appreciated
- Thank you for your comments and suggestions
- Thank your for your creative suggestions
- What a splendid suggestion
- Your suggestions are helpful and welcome

SUMMER
- Have an excellent summer
- You brightened my whole summer
- This one summer holiday I'll never forget
- Your gift will always bring this happy summer back

SUPPORT
- Deeply appreciate your kind support in this matter
- You are always willing to offer support when you can
- Thank you so very much for your continued support
- Any time of the day or night when we need support
- Would like to thank those people and organizations for your support
- Thank you for your advice and support
- You are tremendous source of support and solace
- Our community thanks everyone who came out in support
- Thanks for your repeated support of our fundraising activities
- I wish to thank everyone for their support and kind words
- I would like to thank you for all your support and compassion
- The respect and support you share
- Thanks for your desperately needed support
- In facing such a challenge, your support has been invaluable
- Receiving your support was terrific
- Thank you for your beautiful gesture of support
- Your support means a great deal to me
- Happy to give you our wholehearted support
- Thank you for your comfort and support in my time of trouble
- I know you want nothing in exchange for your support
- Thank you to our foundation support
- Thank you for your generous cooperation and support
- Thanks to everyone who helped and supported

- You continually strengthen our support network
- Really appreciate your ongoing support
- Be assured of our continued support
- You always respect and support your fellows
- Appreciate you unwavering support for us
- Your thoughtful support means so much

Support: uphold, bolster, hold up, boost, prop, relieve, aid, comfort, nourish, maintain, provide for, watch over, tend, nurture, sustain, encourage, advocate, promote, commend, recommend, adopt, shield, protect, defend, validate, affirm, advocate, buoy up, abet, assist, oblige, succor, endorse

See also: CARE, CONTRIBUTE, HELP, SPONSOR

SUPPORTER
- Your very special status as a permanent supporter
- So grateful to supporters like you for making this success possible
- The best supporters come back year after year
- As one of your most dedicated supporters
- In times of trouble, we turn to loyal supporters like you
- Thanks to our supporters, the campaign is a huge success

See also: DONOR, VOLUNTEER, WORKER

SUPPORTIVE
- You have been so supportive, both financially and emotionally
- The most supportive people are often the quietest
- Impossible without supportive neighbors like you
- Thank you for being such a dear and supportive friend
- You have always been one of the most supportive people I know

See also: HELPFUL, KIND

SURE
- I want to make sure you know
- You never wavered from being sure what to do
- You were a sure thing from the start
- You can always be sure of my high regard and affection

SURPRISE
- No one could be more happily surprised
- I was very pleasantly surprised to find out
- Always delights and surprises us
- Very delightfully surprised to hear
- I have never been as surprised in my life

- What a wonderful surprise greeted me
- Imagine our surprise
- Your success is certainly no surprise to us
- Each day brings new discoveries and surprises
- Surprised and delighted

Surprise: astonish, amaze, astound, stun, flabbergast, blow one's mind, overwhelm, overpower, knock for a loop, set back on one's heels, hit between the eyes, take unawares, catch off guard, ambush, come out of nowhere, come like a bolt from the blue
See also: OVERWHELM, SHOCK

SWEET
- How sweet and thoughtful of you
- So very sweet of you to remember
- Sweets to the sweet
- Your sweet nature shines through every day

See also: KIND, THOUGHTFUL

SYMPATHY
- I want to thank you for your kind expression of sympathy
- You sympathy at my loss was greatly appreciated
- Your sympathy did a great deal to help me cope with my problem
- All of us here send our deepest sympathy
- Your note of sympathy meant to much during a difficult time
- Our sympathies on your recent loss
- Wish to thank all our friends and relatives for their thoughtful and compassionate expressions of sympathy

See also: CARE, CONCERN, LOVE

TALENT
- You are so very talented
- Thank you for sharing such talent
- Offering the talent and capabilities that so clearly demonstrate
- You certainly have the talent for finding unique things
- And now your talents shine even more brightly
- Always seeking new talent to enhance
- Your talent and genius produced something magical

See also: ABILITY, SKILL, ACCOMPLISHMENT

TALK
- Thanks so much for talking to me today
- I look forward to talking with you further

- I appreciated the opportunity to talk to you
- I look forward to talking with you again
- Thank you for talking to me in response to my inquiry
- Thank you for talking to me so kindly
- You weren't just all talk and no action

See also: EXPRESS, COMMUNICATION, SAY, SPEAK, WORD

TASTE
- As usual, your taste is exquisite
- As always, everything you did was in the best of taste
- Everything you created was to our taste
- You've given us a magical taste of tropical cuisine
- This is only a taste of all the good things to come

See also: STYLE

TEACH
- You have taught me so much
- Thank you for teaching me the ropes
- There's nothing left to teach you
- You taught me about kindness, hard work, humility and achievement
- You are the one who taught me everything I know

See also: CONTRIBUTE, ENCOURAGE, GUIDANCE, INSPIRE, LEADERSHIP, SHARE

TEAM
- Can always count on team support
- Delighted that the team accomplished so much
- Your team was very disciplined and professional
- You fit so beautifully as a member of our team
- You are such an asset to our team
- Headed a very fine team
- A pleasure to thank the team that gave so much
- Grateful to you individually and as a team

See also: CREW, GROUP, MEMBER, MEMBERSHIP

TELL
- I just wanted to tell you how much it means to us
- Thank you for telling us about this hidden problem
- There's so much I want to tell you
- First, I just have to tell you how much we appreciate

See also: COMMUNICATION, SAY, SPEAK, WORD

THANK

- But first, I have to thank so many of you
- I wanted to thank you as soon as possible
- I just can't thank you enough
- I want to thank you and stay in touch
- I want to publically thank everyone involved
- Thanking our loyal customers with this amazing, limited-time offer
- We have what they'll thank you for
- I do so want to thank all of you
- I wish to thank everyone who pitched in
- I want to thank some specific people for their help
- I want to thank each and every one of you
- Want to thank everyone who has written in and provided insight
- Most of all, I want to thank the backroom workers
- Once again, I have to thank you for
- Thanking all who have helped and contributed
- How can I ever thank you for all you've done for me
- The first order of business is to thank
- We would like to thank the following people
- Your family will thank you again and again
- Just wanted to take a minute to thank you
- I don't know what I can every to thank you enough
- No one grows tired of being thanked
- First and foremost, I want to thank you
- I thank you for your generous help so far
- I would like to thank each of you by name
- Thank you so much for the delightful gift
- Thank you very much indeed
- I look forward to thanking you in person
- Our children's children will thank you fervently
- Thank goodness
- The children thank you
- Kids all around the world will thank you
- To thank you for your support at this time, we want to
- Once again, consider yourself heartily thanked
- For your part in making this possible, I thank you most warmly
- I also want to take this opportunity of thanking you for your support
- On their behalf, I thank you
- It gives me great pleasure to write and thank you for your support
- We put out heads together about the best way to thank you
- If anyone deserves our thanks, it's you
- A difficult task to thank each person individually

- I thank you from the very bottom of my heart
- The committee thanks you in advance for your support and your interest in our cause

Thank: acknowledge, be grateful, give thanks, offer thanks, tender thanks, appreciate, show appreciation, recognize, repay, credit, pay tribute, recompense, return a favor, requite, reward, return

See also: ACKNOWLEDGE, APPRECIATE, CELEBRATE, HONOR, RECOGNIZE, REWARD

THANK YOU

- A little thank you note to
- A really big thank you is needed here
- A special thank you just for you
- A resounding thank you for
- A big thank you to all
- Thank you for standing up for
- Extend a heartfelt thank you from all of us
- It's never too late to say thank you
- Just one more way of saying thank you for choosing
- No matter what you give, thank you for being a friend to
- Oh, thank you
- Once again, thank you for doing your part
- Our way of saying thank you
- Thank you for your patience
- Thank you for your patient response to my questions
- Thank you for allowing us access
- Thank you for checking us out
- Thank you for coming
- Thank you for answering so soon
- Thank you for applying
- Thank you forever
- Thank you for putting up with me
- Thank you from the heart
- Thank you once again for
- Thank you for your feedback
- Thank you all
- Thank you for your correspondence
- Thank you for this shot of realism
- Thank you for fanning the flame
- Thank you to everyone who sent a message
- Thank you for making us your first choice
- Thank you for your order

- Thank you from everyone here
- Thank you for the opportunity to serve you
- Thank you for your business
- Thank you for the pleasant evening
- Thank you for making us your first choice
- Thank you very much for your continued support
- Thank you for whatever you can do to help
- Thank you for being such a good friend last year
- Thank you for being you
- Thank you so very, very much
- Thank you for being a friend of
- Thank you for serving staunchly alongside us
- Thank you for not giving up in the face of overwhelming odds
- Thank you for your interest and support
- Thank you for your caring and ongoing support
- Thank you for standing up for
- Thank you for putting us in a position to benefit all these
- Thank you for your cooperation
- Thank you again for personally helping to make that possible
- Thank you so much for your help
- Thank you for reading my letter; I look forward to hearing from you
- Thank you for your support which is so urgently needed
- Thank you very kindly
- Thank you for really thinking about the causes and solutions
- Thank you from kids everywhere
- Thank you for making a difference in their lives
- Thank you for your consideration
- Thank you for being so generous
- Thank you for your donation which helps prevent disease through research and education
- Thank you so much for increasing your latest donation which means so very much to all of us
- Thank you for so many years of generous support
- Thank you for your unswerving support during these trying time
- There are many ways to say thank you, none of them adequate
- To those of you who can make the extra sacrifice we say a special thank you
- We send a heartfelt thank you to
- We have what they'll thank you for
- Welcome and thank you so much for
- What a difference a simple thank you makes
- Whoever you are, thank you

- With great pride we say thank you to
- You've done so much, I hardly know how to thank you

THANKFUL
- For that, let us be thankful
- I am so thankful for people like you
- If there's one thing for which we can be thankful
- One thing for which we are abundantly thankful
- Thankful not for what you have in your wallet but what you have in your heart
- There's always something to be thankful for
- Deeply thankful for all the good things we have
- Thankful we are living in a country where
- What do you have to be thankful for today
- Whatever your reasons for being thankful
- Those in need are deeply thankful that caring people like you exist

THANKFULNESS
- Thinking of you, I am filled with thankfulness
- Trying to find some way to express my enormous thankfulness
- Every day, I feel so much thankfulness for what you've done
- Thankfulness came welling from the heart

THANKS
- A very special thanks for helping out
- A shower of thanks
- A cartload of thanks
- A truckload of thanks
- A belated thanks for
- A big, big thanks
- A special thanks to all our clients
- A solemn thanks to all those who have given of their time, effort and pocketbooks
- A super thanks to super people
- A proud thanks for making your voice heard
- A personal thanks
- A sincere note of thanks
- Add a note of thanks to those who have volunteered
- Again, my heartfelt thanks for your confidence
- And it's all thanks to you
- As a small token of our thanks
- As you send your donation, please remember these words of thanks

- Bags full of thanks
- Bottomless thanks for just being you
- Bursting with thanks
- But thanks to your timely assistance
- Can you please pass on my thanks
- Convey my personal thanks to everyone
- Extra special thanks
- First, let me send my earnest thanks
- Give more than thanks
- Giving thanks for all that we have
- Heaps of thanks for all your thoughtfulness
- Heartfelt thanks
- Here's a world of thanks
- I know you don't expect thanks
- I want to express my personal thanks for your faith in our organization
- I would like to extend my sincere thanks
- I'm directing my particular thanks to those who
- I'm sending my thanks just for you
- If you have already made a donation early this year, please accept our sincere thanks
- It's our way of saying thanks for being a valued customer
- It's sometimes not easy to say thanks
- It's more than thanks we owe you
- It's our humble way of saying thanks for
- It's customers like you who deserve the biggest thanks
- Just wanted to say thanks
- Just a quick word of thanks
- Trying to think of an even better way to say thanks
- Let us give thanks
- Many thanks to all of you
- Many, many thanks for everything you've done
- Many thanks for your help
- Many thanks for looking after us so well
- More thanks than words can ever say
- My thanks cannot in any way repay you
- My first task in writing you is to express thanks for
- My heart goes out to you in thanks
- On behalf of all those boys and girls your generosity reached, you have my heartfelt thanks
- Once again, a proud thanks for making your voice heard
- Once again, thanks for your support and for speaking up when

- Our heartfelt thanks go out to you as well
- Our company thanks you
- Our thanks come from the very bottom of our hearts
- Please convey my profound thanks to all
- Saying thanks is very special to me
- So long! And thanks
- So worthy of thanks
- Special thanks go out to all participants
- Special thanks spread out across the board to
- Thanks to our product, you never have to
- Thanks for giving your all
- Thanks to all who helped
- Thanks for stopping by
- Thanks for taking a moment to
- Thanks for the valuable information
- Thanks is going out to all those who took time to help
- Thanks for the charming visit
- Thanks for making our lives to rich
- Thanks for a wonderful, enriching experience
- Thanks for the fascinating discussion
- Thanks to all the generous people who shared
- Thanks to our long suffering partners and sponsors
- Thanks for allowing this event
- Thanks, but no thanks
- Thanks for rescuing us
- Thanks be to
- Thanks for the smash hit
- Thanks again for a great time
- Thanks again for the chance to
- Thanks for making so much possible
- Thanks for the brilliant idea
- Thanks for doing your very best
- Thanks a heap
- Thanks a million
- Thanks a lot
- Thanks for taking a moment to make such a difference
- Thanks so much for taking the time to
- Thanks to our crew for
- Thanks for letting me join in
- Thanks to you and yours
- Thanks to the person who did the original work
- Thanks to your foresight and fast action

- Thanks for being such a big help
- Thanks to new technological advances
- Thanks for lending a sympathetic ear
- Thanks for your deeply valued business
- Thanks for putting a smile on so many faces
- Thanks and good wishes
- Thanks for helping recapture the magic
- Thanks for being a true friend
- Thanks for being so cool
- Thanks for the giggle
- Thanks very much for thinking of us
- Thanks for giving me a hand
- Thanks for being one of the good guys
- Thanks for stopping by
- Thanks for the memory
- Thanks for being so upfront
- Thanks for too much to count
- Thanks for putting me back together
- Thanks for making all the pieces fall into place
- Thanks a lot, man
- Thanks for sinking your teeth into this
- Thanks for sharing a glorious day
- Thanks for everything
- Thanks for the magic
- Thanks are long overdue
- Thanks a bunch
- Thanks for your cooperation and perseverance
- Thanks for whatever you can do
- Thanks to the talent and generosity of
- Thanks a whole lot
- Thanks for the help everyone has given
- Thanks for the lift
- Thanks again for making your voice heard
- Thanks again for doing you part
- Thanks to all who gave up their weekend to get this job done
- Thanks for sharing your observations
- Thanks again for choosing us
- Thanks in large part to you
- Thanks to all those who have been active
- Thanks for wanting to know more.
- Thanks for caring so much
- Thanks for signing up

- Thanks for everything
- Thanks for renewing your support
- Thanks to our friends who gave so unstintingly
- Thanks to all of you who helped support this worthy cause
- Thanks for making this vital undertaking such a success
- Thanks for the ride
- Thanks for wanting to be part of this milestone occasion
- Thanks for making everything possible
- Thanks for keeping up the good work
- Thanks for taking care of everything when we couldn't
- Thanks for sharing of yourself so freely
- Thanks for your consideration and support
- Thanks to exciting new leaps forward
- Thanks for your kindness in a stressful time
- Thanks again for making us your first choice
- Thanks for speaking up when every voice means so much
- Thanks to you, our family feels so welcome
- Thanks for thinking of us even in your own time of need
- Thanks for bringing your business to us
- Thanks to your support and encouragement
- Thanks! You really made my day
- Thanks! Come back soon
- The list of thanks is in chronological order
- They'll carry thanks in their hearts for your kindness and generosity
- Very many thanks
- Way cool thanks
- We owe you a big, big vote of thanks
- We can never say thanks often enough
- We extend a very special thanks to
- We owe a humongous thanks to
- We've made it big, thanks to you
- With thanks this week to all our lucky winners
- You inspire heartfelt thanks
- You have our devout thanks
- You deserve so many thanks for

Thanks: tribute, thanksgiving, cognizance, benediction, owing to, because of, due to, as a result of, through, since
See also: THANK, THANK YOU

THINK
- I'm thinking of you right now
- Think of you often with great affection and gratitude

- Always thinking of you
- Thank you so very much for thinking of me
- You really made me stop and think
- I want you to know I'm thinking of you
- Always prodding us to think and learn
- When I think of you, I think of laughter
- Thank you for thinking of us in this special time
- I think of you a lot these days
- Thanks for thinking of us when it counted most
- I think of you especially at this time
- I was thinking of you the other day
- Thank you for thinking of us and sending such nice things

THOROUGH

- You were extremely thorough in explaining the issue
- You certainly gave our business a thorough going over
- I can always count on you for a thorough effort
- When we want a thorough job, we look to you

THOUGHT

- Appreciate your thoughts of us
- I so enjoyed hearing your thoughts and ideas
- Thanks for your unique creative thoughts
- I wanted to share these thoughts with you
- With just a little extra thought, you give so much
- Our fondest thoughts are with you
- Thanks and warmest thoughts
- You put so much thought and care into your gifts
- You are never far from our thoughts
- You are so often in our thoughts
- Comments were well thought out and clearly articulated
- Thank you so much to all who sent positive thoughts
- Special thoughts go out to you
- Warm thoughts are with you from all of us
- Did it with no thought for yourself
- My thoughts are with you as you celebrate

See also: CARE, CONCERN, IDEA, LOVE, ATTENTION

THOUGHTFUL

- One of the most conscientious and thoughtful people I know
- A pleasant and thoughtful person
- Thoughtful people say thanks in a thoughtful way

- Thoughtful enough to carefully evaluate the issues
- Your thoughtful input changed everything
- Your gift was very thoughtfully chosen and just right

THOUGHTFULNESS
- Thanks to your considerate thoughtfulness
- Bowled over by your thoughtfulness
- Again, our thanks for your thoughtfulness
- I will think of you and remember your thoughtfulness
- Thanks for your thoughtfulness and wise advice
- I'll always remember your thoughtfulness
- All deeply touched by your thoughtfulness
- Time and again, I'm amazed at your thoughtfulness and perception
- As always, your thoughtfulness made our day even better

See also: KINDNESS

THRILL
- I was simply thrilled
- So thrilled that your big day has finally come
- Really thrilled to hear about
- I'm thrilled to be able to tell you
- The biggest thrill is your recent achievement
- I feel absolutely thrilled that
- I'm so thrilled for you
- We are thrilled that you are here at last
- We are thrilled to bits for you

See also: DELIGHT, JOY, PLEASURE

THROUGH
- I wouldn't have made it through without you
- You actually followed through
- You always come through for us
- Through thick and thin, you always supported our cause

TIME
- I can't remember when I've had a better time
- I had a lovely time last night
- I know of the many demands on your time
- I want to thank you for all the time you put into
- What a wonderful time we had
- I appreciate the time you gave me last Monday
- I really appreciate that you took the time

- Thanks for taking the time to talk to me
- I thank you most sincerely for your time, energy and enthusiasm
- Thank you for taking time out of your busy day
- Your gift of time and of yourself
- Like to thank all the people who gave so much of their time
- We had the best time
- I know this is an important time for you
- This must be a tough time for you
- This is a time to cherish
- One more time, thanks
- Cannot recall a time when you haven't been there
- Before too much time has gone by
- A great time was had by all
- This is a good time to look ahead
- Thanks for your cheerful support through good times and bad
- This is such a meaningful time
- Though times were not always easy
- It's always a treat to spend time with you
- It's time you had your full due and reward
- You obviously took a lot of time and trouble to
- Looking forward to spending some time together
- Thank you for your time and consideration
- Thank you for taking time from your hectic schedule
- Thank you for your valuable time
- Grateful for your time and careful preparation
- I don't want to take up any more of your time
- Thank you for all the time you devote to
- Thanks for taking the time to inform yourself about

See also: DAY, EVENT, OCCASION. VISIT

TODAY
- I was thinking of you today so I decided to write
- You helped make me what I am today
- All this is possible today because of your hard work
- Today, I am happy to be able to reciprocate
- Today, it's easy to look back on the source of our success

TOGETHER
- Working together, we are unbeatable
- Thanks for pulling it all together
- Together, we did it
- Getting together with you was my smartest move

• You showed us what could be accomplished together

TOKEN
• Presented with the following token of our thanks
• I want to give you this small token of our appreciation
• This humble token cannot begin to show our gratitude
• I would like to hand over a token of my gratitude
See also: AWARD, GIFT, PRESENT

TOUCH
• I am so touched and grateful
• Appreciate all the nice touches you added
• Thanks for adding that special touch
• Whatever you touch turns out right
• You seem to have the magic touch
• You added just the right touches
• You touched my life deeply
• I sincerely hope you will keep in touch
• Let's make a mutual effort to stay in touch
• Gratified and deeply touched by all of your help
• Thanks for remaining in touch
• I am touched deep down inside
• You'll never know how many people you touched
• The best part is keeping in touch with special friends like you
• You truly reflect the common touch
• Will always be in touch with the finer things
See also: FEEL, LOVE, MOVE

TRADITION
• Always in the best and finest tradition
• In keeping with a long and honored tradition
• You've started a whole new tradition here
• It's traditional to show our appreciation by
See also: CELEBRATION, RITE

TREASURE
• I'll treasure it always
• The delight of finding a treasure like you
• I'll forever treasure your gift
• You've turned out to be such a treasure
• Memories of you are the ones I'll treasure most
See also: CHERISH, LOVE, REWARD, VALUE

TREAT
- Provided us with a rare treat
- Thanks for treating us to such an entertaining speech
- Going to the movies with you was such a treat
- Always a treat to listen to you talk
- It was a real treat for me to visit the countryside

See also: **DELIGHT, PLEASURE, REWARD**

TRIBUTE
- Pays well-deserved tribute to
- Paying tribute to fifty years of
- A real tribute to you
- The best tribute we can think of
- A tribute to the virtues you stand for
- The entire program was a tribute to
- As a tribute to our customers, we're offering
- We want to pay tribute to you with this
- A tribute to honor your loyalty and service

See also: **APPRECIATION, GIFT, HONOR, REWARD**

TRIUMPH
- You have certainly scored a triumph
- This is about more than triumph
- Congratulations on a magnificent triumph
- Glad you're adding one more triumph to your achievements
- I look forward to hearing of further triumphs in years to come

See also: **SUCCESS, VICTORY**

TRUE
- Always true to your past and your ideals
- You are a true friend
- You are the true measure of a man
- You had the courage to depart from the tried and true
- Remained true blue right to the end

TWIST
- Never had to twist your arm
- You always managed to put a new twist on the subject
- Our meeting was a very fortunate twist of fate
- Thanks for twisting the tails of the powerful

See also: **CHANCE**

UNDERSTAND
- Nobody listens and understands the way you do
- Make you understand how deeply you are loved and cherished
- Can always count on you to understand
- Right from the very first, you understood what was needed

See also: KNOW, SEE

UNDERSTANDING
- Thanks for being patient and understanding
- Thanks to you, I came away with a keener understanding
- Your comments gave me a good understanding
- Your understanding and support mean such a lot
- Your excellent approach enhanced our understanding
- I deeply appreciated your wise understanding
- Thank you for your assistance and understanding
- My sincere thanks for your understanding

Understanding: comprehension, knowledge, realization, awareness, intelligence, brain power, acumen, astuteness, perspicacity, shrewdness, insight, keenness, enlightenment, sagacity, competence, adeptness, efficiency, capacity

See also: ABILITY, INSIGHT, SKILL, WISDOM

USE
- Will be used frequently
- Know we'll get tons of use out of it
- Think of you each time I use it

USEFUL
- Found all your material very useful
- Such useful advice is not easily found today
- Thank you for providing such useful and informed help
- Your comments were very useful in writing the final report

See also: HELPFUL

VALUE
- You embody the highest values
- Another way to show how much you are valued
- We value you beyond price
- So much about you we value and care about

Value: worth, merit, advantage, benefit, gain, profit, good, significance, standard, ideal, appreciate, venerate, esteem, regard highly, admire,

respect, set great store by, look up to, revere, idolize, cherish, hold dear, treasure, make much of
See also: ADMIRE, CHERISH, ESTEEM, RESPECT

VENTURE
- Grateful you want to help us with these exciting new ventures
- You have devoted a significant portion of your time to this venture
- You gave us the courage to venture out
- You made this venture possible

VICTORY
- Pleased and proud to be part of your victory
- A thrill to claim victory
- This is our victory
- A victory we won by working together
- This victory really belongs to you
- This victory is just beginning

Victory: conquest, success, superiority, mastery, winning, excelling
See also: SUCCESS, TRIUMPH

VISION
- Thank you for your vision
- Gave us all an inspiring vision of how life could be
- Your vision has powerfully shaped this initiative
- We all look to you for a fresh new vision
- You were a vision of loveliness at our party

See also: INSIGHT, WISDOM

VISIT
- Thanks for making our visit so memorable
- You are the main reason we think of our visit so fondly
- Thank you very much for visiting us on the web
- Thanks to all of you who came to visit
- Thank you for visiting our online store
- Your visit was like a shot in the arm
- Thanks for surprising us with your entertaining visit
- We so enjoyed your visit
- I always delight in your visits
- You turned our visit into one of the best ever
- You made our visit a sheer pleasure
- Your visit was a most enjoyable one
- Thank you for visiting us

- Come visit us and see what your donation is doing
- Never realized how much your visit meant

Visit: call upon, look in on, see, look up, come around, stop in, stop by, pop in, turn up, show up, put in an appearance, stay, sojourn, call, stopover

See also: HOSPITALITY, STAY

VOICE

- I would like to add my voice to the many others who support your position
- Together, our combined voices have a powerful effect
- Thanks for standing up for our right to a voice
- No voice has been as strong as yours
- You had the courage to voice your opinions and convictions

See also: COMMUNICATION, SAY, SPEAK, TALK

VOLUNTEER

- Thank you for your hours of volunteer time and financial support
- Our volunteers are the best in the world
- A volunteer like you doesn't come along every day
- With volunteers like you, we'll always come through
- You're the star on volunteer appreciation day
- Thanks for so generously volunteering your time and knowledge
- Thanks to everyone who so graciously volunteered
- Always among the first to volunteer
- Thank you for volunteering so generously
- Thank you to our members and volunteers
- Recognize your volunteer effort on behalf
- Busy as you are, you care enough to volunteer your time

Volunteer: unpaid worker, offer one's services, step forward, step into the breach

See also: DONOR, HELP, SUPPORTER, WORKER

WAIT

- I can't wait to come back
- Finally, all the waiting is over
- Waiting for someone like you to come along
- Now that you are here, the waiting is over
- Because of you, we never had to wait

WAY

- The world's best way to say thank you

- The ideal way to express your thanks and appreciation
- Only one of thousands of ways to say thank
- Now you are really on your way
- The beauty of your gentle, caring ways
- Always something special about the way you do it
- Thanks for going out of your way to help
- I'm especially grateful for the way you took over
- Really liked the way you took charge

See also: CHOICE, PATH

WANT
- I hope you get everything you want
- For a long time, I've wanted to tell you how much I admire you
- The first thing I want to do is congratulate you
- You put aside your own wants in favor of others
- Never could you pass by anyone in want

See also: HOPE, WISH

WARM
- Our warmest wishes go out to you
- Thanks for welcoming us so warmly
- You are one of the warmest people I know
- Holding you in warmest regard
- Wonderful to see you warm up to the challenge

WARMTH
- Your warmth and humor make each work day a delight
- Thank you for your bringing such warmth to our talk
- The warmth of your home made our stay very pleasant
- Your never-failing warmth and friendship make our relationship very special
- You surrounded us with warmth and kindness

See also: AFFECTION, KINDNESS

WELCOME
- We welcome the opportunity to
- Thank you for making me feel welcome
- Thanks for your very friendly welcome
- You made us all feel so very welcome
- Surrounded us with welcome
- What a welcome change you made
- The welcome mat appeared the moment we arrived

- Look forward to welcoming you to our new home

Welcome: greetings, salutations, hello, salute, hail, glad hand, open door, welcome mat, greet, address, meet, usher in, call in, agreeable, pleasing, refreshing, comfortable, enticing

See also: PLEASURE

WINNER

- I know a winner when I see one
- You were a winner from the start
- So glad to have a winner like you on our team
- In this game, we are all winners

See also: LEADERSHIP

WISDOM

- You hold the collective wisdom of our tribe
- Without your wisdom, we would have gone astray long ago
- Hope, one day, to have as much wisdom as you
- Thank you for sharing your wisdom so generously

See also: ADVICE, GUIDANCE, INSIGHT, INSPIRATION

WISH

- With every good wish
- We wish you well in your new venture
- Until I see you again, best wishes
- Wishing you only the finest
- Warmest wishes are coming your way
- May your fondest wishes come true
- I wish you only the best
- I only wish you could have been there to see
- I wish you all success in your endeavours
- Your good wishes are my reward
- Sending you my most affectionate wishes
- I want to express my personal good wishes
- I sincerely wish you well in your future endeavours
- I wish I could have been able to help sooner
- How I wish we could be present
- All good wishes to you
- Every good wish to both of you
- Wish I could be with you at this special time
- Your ingenious gift fulfils my wish for
- You gave me just what I have been wishing for

Wish: desire, yearn, long for, hope, crave, pine, hanker after, eagerness, appetite, preference, fancy, be inclined toward, set one's heart on, relish
See also: HOPE, WANT

WITHOUT
- What would we do without you
- Without you, we couldn't have done it
- I never want to try it without you
- Because of you, no one ever had to go without

WONDER
- I often wonder what we'd do without you
- You're a wonder
- Because of you, we don't have to wonder how we'll succeed any more
- You never have to wonder how much we appreciate you

WONDERFUL
- It's wonderful to be spoiled for a while
- Thanks for being truly wonderful
- I know we will have a wonderful time
- You are really wonderful
- People still tell me what a wonderful experience they had
See also: MARVEL

WORD
- Your kind words helped so much
- Put in a good word for
- There are no words to express what you have done for us
- Thank you for being absolutely true to your word
- You are never at a loss for words
- In facing such a debt of gratitude, I am lost for words
- Thank you for your always thoughtful and comforting words
- It's easy to find words to
- It's very hard to find the words to express
- Words fail me now
- Sincere words express something significant
- A few sincere words can have so much impact
- Even though I'm not good with words
- Your caring words made all the difference
- Thank you for your encouraging words
- Your kind words helped me cope

- All the words have been said in appreciation and thanks
- There truly are no words to adequately express our thanks
- Just a quick word of thanks

Word: talk, speech, pledge, word of honor, vow, guarantee, oath, news, communication, report, scoop, discussion

See also: COMMUNICATE, EXPRESS, PROMISE, SAY

WORK

- We are all very pleased with your work
- Thank you for your hard work and dedication
- A pleasure to work with so many fine people
- Thanks for working so quickly
- Thank you and keep up the good work
- I have long admired your work
- Your work is beautiful
- I have been a fan of your work for many years
- I really enjoyed looking at your work
- I absolutely love your work
- Very pleased with your work
- To honor the high quality of your work
- So that all this hard work will not be in vain
- I know how hard you worked to make this happen
- You have always been so supportive of our work
- Thanks for working under impossible conditions
- I look forward to working with you again
- Keep up the good work
- Your intervention enabled all of us to work together effectively
- Thanks to you, work is proceeding ahead of schedule
- Expressed great interest in working with you
- Look forward to continuing to work with you
- A work of the heart is a work of art
- Working with you makes the day fly by
- Your hard work makes everything so easy for us
- Thank you very much for your excellent work
- Without your hard work we wouldn't have finished in time
- We really count on such help as yours
- I know it was not an easy environment to work in
- You were terrific to work with
- Many thanks for your usual good work
- Thank you for allowing me to work with you

Work: effort, endeavor, exertion, task, job, undertaking, duty, commitment, mission, service, business, occupation, deed, performance, act, operation, achievement
See also: EFFORT, HELP, JOB, SERVICE

WORKER
- An energetic and enthusiastic worker
- One of the best workers in the organization
- Always known as a real worker
- As a worker behind the scenes, you are invaluable
- Wish to recognize one of our most dedicated workers
- Workers like you are immensely valuable

See also: DONOR, SUPPORTER, VOLUNTEER

WORLD
- A world transformed by you
- Bravely facing a world full of challenges
- You make the world a little better
- I believe you really will change the world
- Soon concluded you are going to go far in the world
- People like you make the world a better place to live
- The world is a better, brighter place with you in it
- You opened a new world for me
- You made a world of difference
- Of all the people in my world, you are tops

World: earth, globe, sphere, planet, society, realm, domain, universe

WRITE
- It's about time I wrote to thank you
- The desire to write about this in a personal way
- I wish I could write something clever
- It's hard to write when every word means so much
- Thanks for writing to me out of the blue
- Thank you again for writing such a kind note
- I know I don't always take the time to write
- Though I've thanked you in person, I had to write as well
- How kind of you to write to me
- It was very thoughtful of you to write

Write: inscribe, pen, put pen to paper, jot down, dash off, scrawl, scribble, scratch, compose, author, indite, rhyme, versify, correspond, drop a line, drop a note
See also: COMMUNICATE, TOUCH

YEAR

- Some of the most exciting and productive years of my life
- I hope each of you has a fantastic year
- What a great year we've had because of you
- I hope the next year brings you even more success
- Here's to another great year
- This is a very special time of year
- It's that time of year again
- Look forward to many more wonderful years together
- The years have passed so quickly
- A thanks that lasts all year
- Finally, the culmination of years of planning
- I can't tell you what the past years have meant to me
- I look forward to sharing another wonderful year with you
- Looking forward to doing it again next year
- Thanks for a terrific year
- At this busiest time of year, you worked so hard
- Congratulations on your first fifty years
- Smooth sailing for the years ahead
- Wishing you many happy years to come
- May the passing years bring you much happiness
- Have worked with you happily over the years
- Wishing you all the best in the coming year

See also: TIME

Section Two

Apology

ACCEPT
- Please accept our belated good wishes and sincere thanks
- Please accept our very sincere apology
- I hope you'll accept this very sheepish repentance

ACCEPTABLE
- Please let me know if this is acceptable
- Would really like to make an acceptable restitution
- Renewing our efforts to make our service truly acceptable

ACCIDENT
- You were very kind to say it was an accident
- I agree that this accident was entirely preventable
- In order to make up for this unfortunate accident

ACT
- I'm finally getting my act together
- Truly apologize for how I acted
- Promise to act with more sensitivity in the future
- Acted in a very inappropriate manner
- There is no excuse for how I acted

See also: BEHAVIOR

AMENDS
- Tells us how we can make amends
- Hope there is some way to make amends for what happened
- Make amends at your earliest convenience
- Making amends in the only way we know how

See also: COMPENSATE, FORGIVE, REPAIR, RESTITUTION, SOLUTION

ANSWER
- Sorry I've taken so long to answer your letter
- Answer you in a more acceptable manner
- Certainly we don't always have all the answers
- Will keep at it until we find the right answer

See also: RESPOND

APOLOGIZE
- We apologize for the inconvenience
- Apologize for this regrettable incident
- Sorry, sorry, sorry – I apologize

- Just cannot apologize enough for this catastrophe
- I apologize for adding to your work
- As soon as I discovered the error, I knew I had to apologize
- Cannot apologize too deeply for this oversight
- We apologize for getting back to you so late
- How can I apologize more sincerely
- I want to apologize for taking so long

Apologize: beg pardon, ask pardon, atone for, make up, regret, repent, make amends, lament, rue, eat humble pie, mitigate, palliate, extenuate, justify, excuse
See also: REGRET, SORRY

APOLOGY
- This is my apology in advance
- Please accept our apologies for our absence
- Express personal apologies and regrets to each
- A sincere apology is all I can offer
- You certainly deserve an apology
- I am enclosing my apologies
- A simple apology may not be enough
- I know an apology hardly makes up for my huge error
- Apologies for our regrettable behavior
- This apology is the only the first step in making complete amends

Apology: expiation, confession, repentance, plea, defence, excuse, claim, advocacy, extenuation

ASSURE
- Assure you it will not happen again
- Rest assured that we will take care of the matter
- Hope you are now assured of our sincere intentions

ATTEND
- Sorry that I cannot attend
- Failed to let you know we would be unable to attend
- Unfortunately must attend another function
- How I wish I could attend your wedding
- Sadly must decline your kind invitation to attend

AWARE
- Really should have been more aware of the consequences
- Thank you for making us aware of this problem
- Now aware of how much I have offended

- Please be aware of how contrite I am
- We will certainly be more aware of this problem in the future

BEHAVIOR
- Such behavior is not in keeping with out policies
- Deeply embarrassed by such uncouth behavior
- Want to apologize for my appalling behavior
- Absolutely no excuse for this kind of behavior

See also: ACT

BETTER
- I promise to do better next time
- Really ought to have done better
- What can we do to make this better
- Frank feedback like yours helps us get better

CIRCUMSTANCES
- Explain the circumstances that caused us to disappoint you
- Circumstances refused to cooperate
- More than just a victim of circumstances

See also: SITUATION

COMPENSATE
- Know that nothing can compensate for the frustration and annoyance
- Hope we can compensate by
- Naturally, you will be fully compensated for this

COMPLAINT
- We take every complaint very seriously
- Will act upon your complaint at once
- Have found your complaint a valid one

CONFIDENCE
- Make every effort to restore your confidence in us
- Deeply regret we did not live up the confidence you placed in us
- Let us show you your confidence has not been misplaced

CORRECT
- Will do whatever is necessary to correct the situation
- You observations were correct
- Expect the problem to be corrected very soon

- Please tell us what we can do to correct this error

See also: AMENDS, COMPENSATE, RIGHT

COUNT
- Count on us to make sure it will not happen again
- Hope I can still count you among my dearest friends
- Counting the days until this is put right
- We know how much you were counting on us

CUSTOMER
- Without satisfied customers, our business would vanish
- What can we do to keep you as a valued customer
- As a customer, you are very important to us

DAMAGE
- I feel very bad about the damage
- We will repair any damage immediately
- Hope our reputation has not been damaged permanently in your eyes
- Scrambling to make amends, now that the damage has been done

See also: INCIDENT, PROBLEM, OVERSIGHT, SITUATION

DAY
- I realize we both have had a bad day
- Hope to make amends before the day is out
- Soon be able to forget this day ever happened
- Never thought a day like this could come

DECLINE
- As it is too late, we must sadly decline
- At the last moment, I must decline
- There's no event I hate to decline more
- So sorry to have to decline your kind invitation
- With deepest regrets, we are forced to decline

See also: APOLOGIZE, REGRET, SORRY

DELAY
- I apologize for the delay
- I know that delays caused much frustration
- So sorry for the unnecessary delay
- Won't delay another moment in rectifying the problem
- Promise there will be no such delays in the future

DIFFICULT
- At the moment, it will be difficult for me to
- Sometimes difficult to admit my own shortcomings
- This is a difficult but necessary letter to write
- So sorry for having inadvertently caused such difficulty
- Sometimes it is very difficult to admit we are wrong
- I know I've made the situation more difficult for you

See also: PROBLEM

DISAPPOINT
- Would never intentionally disappoint you
- How disappointed you must feel
- I am as disappointed as you
- Want to apologize for a disappointing performance

DISAPPOINTMENT
- I share your disappointment
- Deeply regret your disappointment
- May you never suffer this kind of disappointment again
- So sorry to cause you disappointment

Disappointment: setback, failure, miscarriage, fiasco, shipwreck, defeat, letdown, disillusionment, chagrin, frustration, bitter pill, sorrow

See also: EMBARRASSMENT, FRUSTRATION

DISMAY
- Imagine my dismay when I realized
- No wonder you were shocked and dismayed
- Dismay is the proper response
- I hope my sincere apology will help you get over your dismay
- News of the error caused great dismay

DISTRESS
- Particularly distressed when a customer feels we have failed to provide services promised
- I can certainly imagine your distress
- Deeply regret having caused you any distress
- Nothing can make up for the distress you have already suffered

EMBARRASS
- You can't imagine how embarrassed I was to discover
- This is a very embarrassing letter to write
- Now I've really embarrassed myself

- For a while, I was too embarrassed even to call
- I don't know which of us was the more embarrassed

EMBARRASSMENT
- Hope I have not caused you embarrassment
- Regret any embarrassment it may have caused
- Apologize for embarrassment to our community

ERROR
- Discovered I was indeed in error
- Mean to rectify the error as soon as possible
- Will whatever we can to erase this error
- Mean to make sure this error never happens again
- Hope you will overlook this unfortunate error

See also: DAMAGE, MISTAKE, OVERSIGHT, PROBLEM

EXCUSE
- Although it was certainly no excuse
- I have no excuse to offer
- I beg you to excuse the offense
- Please accept our excuses

EXPECTATION
- Inform us should our product fail to meet your expectations again
- Regret that I was unable to fulfill your expectations
- You expectations were not too high

EXPENSE
- We will be happy to reimburse your out-of-pocket expenses
- Sorry you have been put to all this expense
- It seems expenses just got out of hand
- Will certainly take care of any extra expenses incurred

EXPLAIN
- Will call tomorrow to explain the unfortunate train of circumstances
- Hope I can explain in a satisfactory manner
- Just can't explain what went wrong
- The more I tried to explain the worse things got

EXPLANATION
- Really have no good explanation
- The explanation offered was not satisfactory

- Want to make sure you are given a full explanation
- I hope this explanation will help you forgive us

FEEL
- No wonder you felt let down
- Will continue until you feel the problem has been solved
- Feel certain we can do much better next time
- No one can feel more remorseful than myself

FORGET
- Horrors! I completely forgot
- How could I have forgotten your birthday
- Really in the doghouse for forgetting
- Once again, I forgot
- I know you won't forget, but I hope you'll forgive
- Hope you will forget the incident ever took place
- I haven't forgotten you
- You must have felt completely forgotten
- I have no excuse; I simply forgot

Forget: lose sight of, cease to remember, draw a blank, overlook, pass over, wink at, neglect, let alone, never mind, leave behind, omit, ignore, disregard, close the eyes to

FORGIVE
- Please forgive me for taking so long
- Very much hope you will forgive me
- Forgive me for being in such a hurry
- To forgive this error is asking a lot

Forgive: absolve, excuse, condone, overlook, make allowances for, pass over, look the other way, waive, indulge, let off the hook, cancel out, delete, erase, reprieve, wipe the slate clean, bury the hatchet, make peace, let bygones be bygones

See also: AMENDS, APOLOGY, COMPENSATE, RECONSIDER, REGRET, SORRY

FRUSTRATION
- I know nothing can make up for the frustration and time lost
- Hope you forgive us for all the frustration caused
- Your frustration was completely our fault
- No wonder you felt so very frustrated

See also: DISAPPOINTMENT, ERROR

GUILTY
- Feel guilty for having let this situation continue
- Look this way to see the guilty party
- Guilty as charged
- Hope you can imagine how guilty we feel

Guilty: culpable, at fault, wrong, illicit, reproachable, blameworthy, amiss, contrite, red-handed, caught with one's hand in the cookie jar
See also: WRONG

HECTIC
- Things have really been hectic
- In the hectic rush, this critical detail has been overlooked
- Got lost in the hectic seasonal activity

HURT
- I can see why you might feel hurt
- Had no intention to hurt you in any way
- What can I do to make the hurt go away
- Unfortunately, some were hurt in the process

See also: DAMAGE. FRUSTRATION

INAPPROPRIATE
- Remarks were inappropriate and do not reflect our beliefs
- My behavior was completely inappropriate
- Quite inappropriate for that setting
- Working to end this inappropriate and embarrassing situation

INCIDENT
- Hope we can put this unfortunate incident behind us
- An incident that didn't need to happen
- Want no more incidents like this one
- Assure you such an incident will not happen again

See also: ACT, BEHAVIOR

INCONVENIENCE
- We apologize for any inconvenience
- The inconvenience was inexcusable
- Want to compensate you for the inconvenience suffered
- Sorry for the difficulties caused by this inconvenience

INQUIRY
- Certainly this matter warrants an inquiry

- According to our inquiries, your complaint is perfectly justified
- Assure you our inquiry will be timely and thorough

INTENTION
- My intentions were the best
- Sometimes the best intentions go awry
- Realize that good intentions are not enough
- It is our intention to rectify the deviation as soon as we can

KNOW
- I don't know what got into me
- If only we had known about the difficulty
- Really should have known better
- Please know that we did not foresee this event
- Didn't know it would come out this way

LUCK
- Just my luck that I must miss you
- Hope to turn this bad luck into good
- Determined to turn our luck around
- We admit this was more than just rotten luck

Luck: chance, serendipity, happenstance, fortune, lot, fate, fluke, contingency, accident, how the ball bounces, how the cookie crumbles

MAKE
- You must let me make it up to you
- Will do just about anything to make it better
- It's time to make amends
- So you won't have to make do any more

See also: AMENDS, COMPENSATE

MESS
- So sorry for my part in this mess
- I really messed up this time
- Will take care of this mess very speedily
- Promise to clean up this messy problem pronto

See also: EMBARRASSMENT, INCONVENIENCE, PROBLEM

MISTAKE
- Once again, I'm sorry for the mistake
- Hope you will forgive the mistake on my part
- Will attempt to rectify any mistakes

- Promise not to make the same mistake again
See also: ERROR, FRUSTRATION, OVERSIGHT

MISUNDERSTANDING
- Profoundly regret our recent misunderstanding
- Discover it has all been a sad misunderstanding
- So easy for misunderstanding to develop
- Intend to trace this misunderstanding back to its cause

NOTHING
- I know nothing can make up for
- There is nothing I won't do to change this
- Nothing I can say or do can erase
- Make sure all our efforts haven't been for nothing

Nothing: naught, none, diddly squat, no clue, nix, zilch, not a scrap, no hint, *nada*

OBLIGATION
- Fully recognize our obligation to
- Thank you for pointing out our obligation in this matter
- Now under even greater obligation to you

Obligation: necessity, promise, duty, requirement

OVERSIGHT
- Will correct this oversight at once
- I assure you this oversight was not intentional
- Hope you will forgive this oversight
- Please know that we are working to remedy this oversight at once
- To think, this all began with a perfectly innocent oversight

See also: APOLOGY, DAMAGE, ERROR, FORGIVE, GUILTY, MISTAKE, REGRET, SORRY

PERSONAL
- Personally dispatched a staff member to look into the matter
- Cannot personally attest to
- Realize that this oversight has affected you personally
- Will take personal responsibility for this disaster

POINT
- You are quite right to point out
- So glad you pointed out the error
- Hope to turn things around at this point

- Really has gone beyond the point of no return

PRIDE
- Take pride in our work and are particularly distressed when
- Until now we've taken great pride in our efficiency
- I can understand just how your pride was wounded
- I'm putting my pride totally aside
- Want to restore our pride in a trouble-free operation

PROBLEM
- To ensure this problem will not recur
- Responsibility for this problem is entirely our own
- Promise to clear up this problem immediately
- Despite our best efforts, this problem keeps popping up
- This is one problem that won't happen again

See also: FRUSTRATION, ERROR, INCONVENIENCE, MISTAKE, OVERSIGHT

PROVE
- Only proves we are both stubborn
- Let us prove we've really changed
- Now is the time for us to prove otherwise
- Please give us another chance to prove our worth

RECONSIDER
- I hope you will please reconsider
- Ask that you reconsider your position
- Please reconsider your decision to
- I beg you to reconsider

See also: FORGIVE

REGRET
- I immediately regretted my hasty action
- Regret to inform you I must withdraw
- Hard to tell you just how much I regret
- First, let me express my profound regret for this incident
- It is with particular regret I must decline
- I regret we will be unable to attend
- I'd like to express my sincere regrets
- My only regret is that I couldn't thank you sooner

See also: APOLOGY, GUILTY, SORRY

REPAIR

- Do whatever it takes to repair our relationship
- Will make all the necessary repairs free of charge
- I want to repair your broken heart
- Working to repair everything that is damaged between us

RESPOND

- Sorry I have been such a slow poke in responding
- Should have responded to you much earlier
- Wanted to respond right away to your dissatisfaction
- You responded with justified criticism

See also: ANSWER

RESPONSE

- Obviously most unsatisfactory in failing to reach response targets
- Apologize for any delayed response
- The response should have been much faster

RESTITUTION

- Just tell me how I can make restitution
- Of course, full restitution goes without saying
- Plan complete restitution as soon as possible

See also: AMENDS, COMPENSATE, REPAIR, SOLUTION

RIGHT

- Now appears that you were right all along
- Plan to do right by you no matter what it takes
- Finally see that it is the right thing to do
- Will work very hard to make things right with you
- It's certainly time to right this wrong
- So determined to be right that I didn't listen to you

See also: CORRECT

SATISFY

- Will not be satisfied until I return it to its original condition
- Will do everything we can to satisfy you
- Won't stop until you are completely satisfied
- Our aim is to send every patron home satisfied

Satisfy: gratify, please, content, appease, gladden, resolve, solve, persuade, reassure, pacify, placate, fulfill, answer, assure, compensate, reimburse, atone for, make reparation, pay back

SERVICE
- Sorry to learn our response to your service needs disappointed you
- Will work harder to improve this service in the future
- You are certainly entitled to better service than this

SITUATION
- Will reevaluate the situation at once
- Do our very best to change this unhappy situation
- Very sorry for allowing this unfortunate situation to develop
- Never thought to find ourselves in a situation like this

SOLUTION
- Value your business and hope this solution is satisfactory
- Let's work toward a solution together
- For a solution we can all live with
- A speedy solution to this impasse is called for
- After several tries, I think I've finally found a solution

See also: AMENDS

SORRY
- Very sorry to hear about
- So sorry to hear you have been taken ill
- Very sorry to hear a member of our staff was rude
- Extremely sorry to lose you
- So sorry for the times I let you down
- First, let me say how sorry I am
- You'll never be sorry
- Sorry! We'll be right back
- We're sorry
- I'm so sorry to have to do this
- Sorry to take so long to congratulate you
- Sorry to learn of your recent troubles
- So sorry you weren't able to share our day
- So sorry we can't be there to celebrate with you

Sorry: guilty, repentant, apologetic, abject, humbled, rueful, remorseful, chastened, sheepish, embarrassed, distressed, dejected, downcast, crestfallen

See also: APOLOGIZE, EMBARRASS, GUILTY, REGRET

STEP
- Taking steps to ensure it never happens again
- Should have taken that step long ago

- One more step on the road to reconciliation
- If we each take a step, we'll meet in the middle

See also: ACT

TELL

- Thank you for telling us of your dissatisfaction
- As soon as you told us, we went into action
- Only wish you had told us sooner
- Want to tell you how sorry I am
- Don't know what to tell you, except to apologize again

THANKS

- Again, my thanks and apologies
- Thanks for being so understanding
- Convey our thanks for all your patience
- A time when thanks is just not enough
- Apologize for not thanking you right away

TOUCH

- Sorry I haven't kept in touch
- I know I'm really late getting in touch with you
- Promise to keep in touch from now on
- This won't happen again, touch wood
- If I had kept in touch, this problem wouldn't have happened

TRY

- I will try my very best to
- Will try to do better in the future
- There's nothing for it but to try harder
- When trying is just not good enough
- Promise to keep trying until I succeed

Try: attempt, undertake, seek, venture, aim, strive, struggle, bend over backward, push, test, experiment, prove

See also: PROVE

UNFORGIVABLE

- Completely unforgivable to have behaved like that
- Such bad service is unforgivable
- This was an unforgivable error
- Hoping you will forgive the unforgivable
- An unforgivable injustice has just been committed
- Hope this act is not permanently unforgivable

Unforgivable: inexcusable, unpardonable, unjustifiable, scandalous, unwarranted, reprehensible, deplorable, low, atrocious, beastly, odious, disgraceful, shameful, despicable
See also: DAMAGE, MISTAKE, WRONG

UNFORTUNATE
- Unfortunately, I've just become redundant
- Working hard to change this unfortunate problem
- A very unfortunate situation all round
- Nothing could have been more unfortunate than this

See also: HURT, UNHAPPY

UNHAPPY
- Just very sorry you are unhappy with
- Pains us to know you are unhappy with the service
- Cannot afford even one unhappy customer
- I'm very unhappy to learn you are unhappy

See also: UNFORTUNATE

VALUE
- Value your friendship too much to
- Can't put a value on how much you mean
- Please accept this item of increased value in compensation
- Really don't want to lose value in your eyes

WISH
- Certainly wish this had never occurred
- Really wish to patch things up
- Wishing so hard that I had paid more attention
- Dearest wish is for us to be friends again
- Wouldn't wish this on anyone, must less a friend like you

WORD
- Find us at a very distressing loss for words
- Sadly, we did not live up to our word
- Words can hardly convey how upset I feel
- Deeply regret going back on my word

WORK
- Hope we can work this out together
- This time we are determined to make it work
- Have been working to fix it since the moment we found out

- We're working on this as fast as we can
- Work very hard to make this right
- For a long time, thing just haven't been working between us

WRITE
- Writing to say how sorry I am for what happened
- Taking this opportunity to write and apologize
- Please forgive me for not writing sooner
- This is the hardest letter I've ever had to write

Write: pen, inscribe, jot down, dash off, scribble, compose, note
See also: INFORM

WRONG
- Will use whatever power we possess to right this wrong
- Ready to admit I was wrong
- According to the proverb, two wrongs don't make a right
- Completely wrong to insist
- I now realize I couldn't have been more wrong
- Do everything possible to wipe out this wrong
- Clearly, you have been wronged

See also: ERROR, MISTAKE

YEAR
- Hard to believe a whole year has passed
- Apologize for letting another year go by without
- Hope to put this troubled year behind us
- This certainly has been a year for misunderstandings
- Let's make this a year of reconciliation

Section Three

Condolence

ALONE
- You surely know you are not alone in this
- But you will not be going through this tragic time alone
- At a time like this, you are never alone
- He fought for what was right, even if he had to fight alone

APPRECIATE
- Appreciate your thoughts at this difficult time
- Appreciate how much you have lost
- Appreciate having your family around you at a time like this
- Makes each of appreciate what is truly important in our lives
- Learned to appreciate her gentle, humble side

ASSISTANCE
- Please be assured that any assistance you require is at your immediate disposal
- If I can render any assistance at all, please call
- Every assistance is yours for the asking

BEREAVE
- Our hearts go out to all those who have been bereaved
- Bereaved of a loved one far too early in life
- How sad to be so tragically bereaved
- Your whole family has been very sadly bereaved
- Understand what it is to be bereaved of one's nearest and dearest

BEREAVEMENT
- Offer you our deepest sympathies in your sad bereavement
- Your friends and family are around you in your bereavement
- Your bereavement is shared by the whole community
- Know how deeply we feel for you in your bereavement

BOND
- Connected by a deep bond of sympathy
- Shared a bond that only grew stronger over the years
- Will reinforce bonds already powerful
- The breaking of such a loving bond is always shattering

BURDEN
- Willingness to share the burden
- Little we can say to alleviate the terrible burden
- While we cannot ease the weight of your burden

- So sorry that this burden has fallen upon you
- With all our support, your burden will grow lighter

CALL
- Please feel free to call on me at any time
- I will call to express my sympathies in person
- Suddenly called to a different place
- Just call, and I'll be at your side

CARE
- Take care and hurry back
- Take good care of yourself
- Don't have to tell you how much I care
- We care about you very much
- Please take extra care of your own personal needs
- Others care and share in your loss
- Was deeply caring about everyone

COMFORT
- Draw some measure of comfort from knowing others care
- The nearness of friends and family will comfort you
- No words that can offer comfort at this sad time
- Take comfort in your memories in this moment of sadness
- We will do all we can to give you comfort

CONCERN
- Wanted to let you know how concerned we all are
- Deeply concerned about you right now
- You stand first in our concerns

CONDOLENCE
- Please accept our sincere condolences
- On behalf of the entire family, I would like to offer our condolence
- Extend my condolences to your and your family
- You know our condolences are deeply felt
- Offer sincere condolences for your heartbreaking loss

CONTRIBUTION
- Made so many significant contributions
- Impossible to summarize her impressive contribution
- Appreciate his enormous contribution

COUNT
- You can count on me for whatever you need
- Was someone we all counted upon
- So proud to have been counted among her friends
- Was a person who really counted in the world

DAY
- Better days are ahead for all of us
- This is a very sad day indeed
- Always knew this day would come
- Look forward to the day when you can smile again

DEATH
- Sudden death took us all by surprise unexpected
- So very sorry to hear of this unforeseen death
- With deep regret, I am compelled to note the death
- It's always a shock, even when death is expected

DEPLORE
- Much reason to deplore his passing
- Deeply deplore this tragic accident
- Sad at the very deplorable outcome

DISASTER
- Together, we will work through this disaster
- Her loss is a disaster to us all
- This disaster powerfully affects us all
- Must grow stronger in times of disaster like this

DONATION
- Please consider a donation to her favorite charity
- Appreciate a donation to a worthy cause
- Would have been very pleased by a donation to

EXPRESS
- Would like to express our heartfelt condolences to you
- Expressing the deep feelings this event stirs up
- Wish I could express how much I feel her loss
- These words can't come close to expressing what I feel

FAMILY
- With particular thoughts to your family

- Times like this draw families closer together
- Now is when you need your family near
- Was always so proud of her family
- Heart goes out to family and friends
- Now someone precious is missing from the family circle

FAVORITE
- A great favorite among us
- Mourn the loss of one of my very favorite people
- Was always my favorite relative
- Made me feel I was her favorite person

FEEL
- Can only imagine how you are feeling
- Feelings of sympathy are deeply appreciated
- Understand how you feel right now
- Come to feel I had found a friend I admired
- Her loss will be felt by all of us
- All of us feel for you in your loss

FOND
- Our fond respects are with you
- Always very fond of the deceased
- Comforted by so many fond memories
- It was always clear how fond she was of you

FOREVER
- The wonderful memories will be with us forever
- Thought he would be with us forever
- Will be forever in our hearts

FRIEND
- Hope you will draw strength from your many friends
- Friends who want to help you get through this time
- Will try to be an even better friend in your time of need
- Know that you have many loyal and caring friends
- Feel we have lost a friend and a voice for the less fortunate
- Lost a friend I could always look to for inspiration

GOODBYE
- It is very difficult to say goodbye
- Hope we can say goodbye together

- We want to help you say goodbye
- The time has come when we must say goodbye

GRIEF

- Your grief is our grief
- Know that no one can truly share your grief
- Eventually this grief will fade
- Share your grief in these dark hours
- Share the grief and sense of loss

GRIEVE

- The period of grieving will be difficult for you
- We all grieve the loss
- Know we are with you as you grieve
- The entire community will grieve
- It's only natural that you grieve

HEART

- Embrace you in our hearts
- Cannot express all that is in our hearts
- Our hearts are deeply moved
- My heart goes out to you
- This loss will leave a deep void in our hearts

HELP

- Want so much to help you if I can
- Hope I may help you in some way at this difficult time
- Please know that we are ready to help in any way
- I hope these words of condolence will be of help

HOPE

- Hope you are on the mend soon
- In this dark time, hope for the future still shines through
- Hope you will turn to us
- Want to assure that hope and comfort will return for you
- Hope in this dark hour of suffering and uncertainty

INSPIRATION

- Was an inspiration to us all
- The inspiration he provided changed my own life
- Her leadership and inspiration led us to undreamed heights

INTRUDE
- Do not wish to intrude upon your solitude
- Hope I am not intruding
- If I'm intruding in any way, please tell me

JOIN
- Please join us in remembering
- Join you in your sorrow
- Now is the time for all of us to join together
- Join with others to get through this together

KNOW
- Feel as if we knew her personally
- Through your wonderful stories, we all felt we knew him well
- Want to let you know how very much my sympathy goes out
- So glad I had a chance to know her
- Lucky enough to have known her well

LIFE
- Thank you for being part of her life
- Our lives have been changed forever
- His life will remain an inspiration
- Loss of life in tragic circumstances
- Will have an enormous impact on all our lives
- Accomplished so much in a shortened life

LISTEN
- Here to listen if you need to talk
- Always willing to listen
- At a time like this, listen to your heart
- Listened to everyone's point of view

LOSS
- The news of your loss has saddened us
- While no words can ease your loss
- Making the loss felt all the more keenly
- A great loss for all of us
- Reaching out to help you in your tragic loss
- An immense loss to the public
- This loss has shaken us to our foundations
- This is indeed a tremendous loss
- Still in shock for the loss of such a dear person

- Such a loss defies understanding

LOVE
- Trust the memory of her love will give you strength
- Someone who was deeply loved and will be deeply missed
- Loved by all who had the pleasure of knowing her
- His love for his fellow citizens took him to a peak of achievement
- Was loving, generous and compassionate

LOVED ONE
- You have always spoken highly of your loved one
- Deepest sympathies to all who lost a loved one
- The loss of a loved one is always a terrible blow
- Nothing is more precious than our loved ones

MEMORIAL
- Going forward is the best memorial
- Her memorial is the love she leaves in our hearts
- A splendid memorial to an extraordinary person
- A donation to a charity of your choice is a fitting memorial

MEMORY
- So many memories we will always cherish
- Cherish the memories the two of you shared
- Memories will help ease your pain
- Memories we treasure now more than ever
- Alive in the memory of all who knew her
- Memories are a source of great joy
- Has been part of so many happy memories
- In honor of their memory, courage and dedication
- Happy memories of the wonderful years you spent together

MESSAGE
- A message of encouragement and support
- Joining the many other messages of sympathy
- This message comes to you from many caring people

MISFORTUNE
- Heart goes out to you in your sad misfortune
- No greater misfortune that the loss of a loved one
- So sorry this misfortune has visited you

MISS
- Will be missed by all
- You will be much missed while you recover
- Will be very sadly missed
- We miss her too
- I miss her so very much already
- We miss him a lot
- Now someone very dear is missing from our community

MOURN
- Share your grief and mourn with others for this loss
- We mourn with you
- Faith that, after the mourning, hearts begin to heal
- In the days of mourning ahead, we are there for you

NEED
- Let us know if there's anything you need
- Whatever your needs, just ask
- Need the support of your dear ones right now

NEWS
- Thank you for sharing this news with me
- Was deeply dismayed by the news
- The news that no one wants to hear
- Place on record our sorrow at the news

OFFER
- Can offer little except my sincere wishes for your comfort
- If I can offer any help or comfort
- Always had to much to offer her community
- Always one of the first to offer his services

OUTLOOK
- Help most by keeping an optimistic outlook
- Please do not allow this to change your warm outlook on the world
- Our outlook has forever changed

OWN
- Felt was almost our own
- Hurts most to lose one of our own
- The whole community mourns one of its own

PEACE

- A way to find peace in your heart and a way forward
- May he rest in peace
- Work through grief to a place of peace
- Hope that peace will soon surround you

PERSON

- Admired and loved him as a person
- A person of rare vision and inspiration
- A person with so much left to do
- So privileged to have known such a person
- Was a good friend and a good person

PERSONAL

- Though I was not personally acquainted with
- Wanted to write to you personally to tell you
- A loss like this is so deeply personal
- Miss her personal warmth and friendship most of all

PROMISE

- Please promise to let us know how you are
- Now is a time to keep promises of friendship and love
- Showed such shining promise right from the start
- A very promising career has been cut short
- A comfort to know such a promising life has been fulfilled

READY

- Want to see you when you are ready for visitors
- Stand ready to help at any moment
- Was always ready take time to listen
- Take time to heal and return to work when you are ready

REGARD

- Held her in high regard because of her selfless and untiring commitment
- Always held you in such tender regard
- Regarded her as a second mother
- He regarded me as a protege and gave me so much invaluable help

REGARDS

- Please extend my personal regards to your family
- Sending you deepest regards at this sad time

- Everyone here sends you sincere regards

REGRET
- Extend our sincerest regrets and sympathies
- Deeply regret this unfortunate loss
- It is with much regret I learned of this unhappy event

REMARKABLE
- What a remarkable individual she was
- What a remarkable person to have such devoted friends
- Was remarkable in every way

REMEMBER
- Remembered with respect and admiration
- Will always remember her wicked sense of humor
- So glad we have something precious to remember her by
- Will remember his kindness every day

REPLACE
- An inspirational leader impossible to replace
- No one can replace her
- Who could replace such a special person
- Will never be replaced in our hearts

SAD
- So very sad to hear the news
- A very sad day has come
- Will be all the sadder for her absence
- On this sad occasion we send you our deepest respects
- Know you will be sad for a long time
- So sad that we will not see him again

SADDEN
- Were saddened by her passing
- Particularly saddened by his loss
- Your loss saddens all of us
- Shocked and saddened to learn of the expected passing
- Your loss has deeply saddened your friends and neighbors

SADNESS
- Support you during this time of sadness
- It is with great sadness that I heard about

- Provide a smile in the midst of this sadness
- Share the pain and sadness

SHARE
- Have shared many pleasant times with
- Know that we share your grief
- All of us share a deep sense of loss
- Share the feeling of losing a member of the family

SHOCK
- The news came as a tragic shock
- Shocked to learn the sad news
- Such a loss is always a big shock
- Do whatever we can to help you over the shock
- Shocked and saddened by these events
- Shocked and grief-stricken to hear about the terrible accident
- Found myself in a state of shock

SINCERE
- Offer sincere, heartfelt condolences on your tragedy
- Was always refreshingly sincere in her desire to help
- A sincere desire to help you through this
- Felt such sincere affection for her
- A deeply sincere person in all that he did

SORROW
- An expression of sorrow and support
- Know we are with you in your sorrow
- This sorrow too will pass
- In your time of sorrow, we want so much to help
- With deepest sympathy and sorrow
- My sympathy goes out to you in your great sorrow
- The mark of sorrow is seen on every face
- Express our profound sorrow and heartfelt condolence

SORRY
- So sorry to hear you are ill
- Sorry this happened to such a wonderful person as you
- Our whole family is sorry to learn of your unfortunate accident
- Very sorry to learn about your tragic loss
- All of us are deeply sorry that such a wonderful person is gone

SPECIAL

- The deceased was very special to us
- Always hard to lose such a special person
- Special to everyone who knew her
- Always had a special place in our hearts
- Remember all the special time you had together

STEADFAST

- Remain steadfast in our solidarity
- Was the most steadfast of friends
- Her steadfast leadership guided us for years

STORY

- I'm sure you have many delightful stories to tell about
- Now we have come to the end of the story
- Has such an inspiring life story to tell
- His life story provides a shining example we would do well to follow

STRENGTH

- Give you special strength and comfort
- Know you have the strength to get through this
- Find inner strengths you didn't know you had
- Was always a tower of strength to those around her

SUPPORT

- Support for a grieving friend, colleague or loved one
- Care about you and want to offer my support
- Stand ready to render all possible support
- Will never forget her warm support and kind help
- Support has been an inspiration to us all

SUSTAIN

- Hope the care and concern of your friends will sustain you
- Help to sustain you in the difficult days ahead
- Call upon deep resources to sustain you

SYMPATHY

- Please convey my sympathy to her spouse and children
- We send you our sympathy at this trying time
- Our sympathies are with you
- Wish to convey our deepest sympathy upon the loss

- Express my sympathy for those who mourn

TEARS
- When tears give way to smiles again
- Help you smile through your tears
- When the tears are done, you will remember fondly
- Tears are being shed in many places
- Shed tears at this upsetting news

THINK
- Know that I'm thinking of you
- Can't think of him without remembering so many good times
- Will think of you every day as you go through this
- Please think of the many friends who surround with love

THOUGHT
- Our thoughts are with you at this time of sorrow
- You have never been far from our thoughts
- Your thoughts and wishes are very valuable to us
- Never thought this day would come

TIME
- Hope that time and memories will lessen the burden of your sorrow
- Your perseverance during this difficult time
- This sad time, too, will pass
- Through our tears, we'll remember the good times
- Still have fond memories of our times together

TRAGEDY
- This tragedy has caused unspeakable grief and sorrow
- Very sad to hear that tragedy has visited you
- Very sorry to hear about this tragedy
- Extend our sympathies to those directly affected by this tragedy
- Trust we will emerge all the stronger from this tragedy
- We were all stricken by this tragedy

TREASURE
- Will always treasure the memories
- Have lost a treasured member of our group
- Treasure her achievements all the more
- A great treasure has been lost

TROUBLE
- Very sorry to learn of your recent troubles
- This trouble too will pass
- Your unexpected trouble concerns us very much
- Stand beside you in this time of trouble

TRUST
- We trust the memory will comfort you
- Put your trust in the love of those around you
- Was one of our most trusted friends and colleagues

TURN
- Confident everything will turn out just fine
- Now is the time to turn to friends and family
- You can always turn to us for help and comfort
- This shocking turn of events has deeply saddened us

VALUE
- Know how much you valued your dear one
- Such a valued member of our community will be sorely missed
- I valued every moment I was privileged to spend with
- Deeply valued his friendship and personal warmth

VISIT
- Distance precludes a personal visit
- Plan to visit you as soon as you feel ready
- Sooner or later, sorrow visits all of us

WORDS
- No words adequate to ease the burden of your grief
- Means more than I can express in words
- Words cannot express how deeply grieved I was to hear
- While no words can erase your loss, let me say

WRITE
- It is with great sorrow I am writing to tell you
- Difficult to write with such unhappy news
- Nothing I can write will ease your pain
- It is with great sympathy that I write this note
- One of the hardest letters I've ever had to write

Section Four

Exclamations

Signatures

EXCLAMATIONS

- Together, we did it!
- Hey there!
- We really appreciate it!
- You are perfect!
- Sorry! We'll be right back!
- Ready made!
- Ready for you!
- Always ready!
- Totally amazing!
- Get ready for savings!
- Come for a visit!
- Warmest appreciation!
- We're sorry!
- Thanks to all!
- You are the best!
- Oh thank you!
- Huzzah for you!
- Warmest thanks!
- Extra special thanks!
- Thanks a heap!
- Thanks for visiting us!
- Thank you forever!
- Thanks a bunch!
- A big thank you!
- Consider this a hug!
- Grateful forever!
- Deeply in your debt!
- Thanks a lot!
- Celebrate!
- Pat yourself on the back!
- Thanks a million!
- A big thanks!
- Thank you all!
- You made it!
- Hooray!
- Thank you, thank you, thank you!
- What a gift!
- What an accomplishment!
- Keep up the good work!

- Peachy keen!
- We knew you could!
- So long! And thanks!
- Thanks! Come back soon
- You delivered!
- You've got what it takes!
- My cup runneth over!
- Awesome!
- Loved every minute!
- Behind you all the way!
- Marvellous!
- We adore you!
- Wow!
- Astounding!
- You're a walking marvel!
- Over the moon!
- Gob smacked!
- I can't believe it!
- Hear, hear!
- Well done!
- Brilliant performance!
- I'm so impressed!
- Many happy returns!
- You've done it again!
- Hats off to you!
- Excellent show!

SIGNATURES

- Admiringly yours
- Affectionately yours
- Affectionately
- All my love
- All the best
- Best regards
- Best wishes
- Bless you during this
  beautiful spring season

- Bless you for your gift of compassion
- Bless you
- Cheers
- Cheerfully yours
- Cordially
- Cordially yours
- Faithfully
- Fondly
- For the love of kids
- Goodbye for now
- Gratefully yours
- Happy anniversary
- Happy birthday
- Hugs and kisses
- In fellowship and love
- In gratitude
- In deepest friendship
- Keep me posted
- Kind regards
- Kindest regards
- Look forward to seeing you
- Love to all
- Love
- Love and kisses
- Many thanks
- Many thanks ane warm regards
- Our deepest affection to you
- Peace be with you
- Peacefully yours
- Regards
- Remembering you
- Respectfully
- Respectfully yours
- See you later
- Sincerely
- Sincerely yours
- Thank you
- Thank you for helping
- Thank you
- Thanks sincerely
- Thanks in advance
- Thinking of you
- Very truly yours
- Very sincerely yours
- Very cordially yours
- Very gratefully yours
- Very truly yours
- Warm regards
- Warmest personal regards
- Warmly yours
- Wishing you every success
- Wishing you all the best
- Wishing you success
- Wishing you the very best
- With best wishes
- With great interest
- With deepest sincerity
- With thanks
- With deepest love and affection
- With special thoughts
- With much love
- With deepest respect
- Your friend always
- Your friend
- Your friend for life
- Yours in the future of health care
- Yours in thanksgiving and loyalty
- Yours for a fairer future
- Yours in truth
- Yours truly
- Yours sincerely
- Yours in loyalty
- Yours faithfully
- Yours forever
- Yours in peace

Section Five

Sample
Letters

CLUB SPEAKER

Dear Mr. Spreen,

Thank you for agreeing to speak to our club. We can hardly wait for your arrival. All of our members have a very keen interest in railway history and look forward to hearing your experiences with the last operational steam engines.

Many of our club members remember the such engines from their youth. The younger rail enthusiasts are eager to pepper you with questions.

I have enclosed directions to our meeting place and I will call beforehand to see if there is any other way I can help.

Best regards,

Bob Mogolis
Chief Engineer

EMPLOYEES

Dear Fellow Workers,

I would certainly like to be able to thank each one of you by name. However, this project involved the efforts of over three hundred people so I can only express my collective gratitude for all the hard work that brought us this success.

I especially want to recognize project management heads who kept the entire undertaking on time and within budget. The construction team did a splendid job and the advance placement team came through magnificently too. And, of course, none of it would have been possible without our energetic marketing group who brought in the original orders.

The skill of so many went into the successful completion. I hope each one of you understands just how much the entire company is indebted to you for the great showing this year.

Thank you again for a stellar performance.

Sincerely,

Asta Swenton
President

JOB INTERVIEW

Dear Ms. Wardle:

It was a pleasure meeting you Tuesday. I very much enjoyed learning more about your Youth Program. Your team has accomplished an impressive amount in a very short time.

I find the prospect of working with you very exciting. My part time jobs and internship last summer at the Step Up initiative for teenagers have given me an excellent picture of your requirements. I feel strongly committed to work in this field.

I shall wait with anticipation during your search period. Please do not hesitate to call if you need any further information.

Many thanks for your consideration.

Respectfully,

Mary Harrison

REFERENCE

Dear Ms. Harrison:

I want you to know how much I appreciate the letter of reference you provided to include with my resume.

Your recommendation was the deciding factor in the decision of Millar and Company to hire me. It is my dream job. I'll be working with a number of people very skilled in my chosen field and the opportunities to learn are enormous. I can hardly wait to begin.

Thank you so much for helping a young person like me get such a terrific start.

Yours truly,

Gilda Parks

LETTER OF INTRODUCTION

Dear Peter,

I just want to let you know how grateful I am for the letter of introduction you wrote to Angela Whitely on my behalf.

Yesterday, I joined her for a breakfast meeting. She mentioned you warmly and has decided to accept me as one of her choreography students. As you well know, I have been searching for a mentor of her calibre ever since I graduated from Magran's advanced dance program last spring.

Let me know when you are free. I want to take you out to dinner to celebrate the rare honor Ms. Whitely has conferred – thanks to your recommendation.

And, of course, you will be my guest at the first performance to involve my work.

Gratefully yours,

Inga

INTERVIEW FOLLOW UP

Dear Mr. Dean

Thank you for the opportunity to discuss your position for a customer relations specialist. I enjoyed meeting both you and other members of the department and learning about the company's planned initiatives in the western district.

In particular, I was impressed with the three new stores now under construction. They are needed to serve the communities rapidly growing around them. Your strong commitment to both employee and customer satisfaction will certainly build a loyal staff and consumer base. As I have a keen interest in the development of retail services in these communities, I would welcome the opportunity to be part of your growth in this area by working at your company.

I believe my degree in marketing and my experience working with customer profiling at Y. Y. Yaggers for two years qualify me for the position. In addition, my knowledge of the newest profiling software would be a valuable asset for your firm.

I look forward to hearing from you soon. In the meantime, please call me if I can answer any additional questions or provide more information.

Yours faithfully,

Julian P. Grover

SERVICE TO CLUB OR ORGANIZATION

Dear Mary,

You have given generously of your time, energy and talents to the Markle Street Parkette Committee. We would like to thank you for everything you have done to make the Parkette project such a success.

From the beginning, your enthusiasm carried us through, even when it looked as though that bit of wasteland covered with construction rubble could never be reclaimed. You never gave up once. Now, mainly due to your hard work and enthusiasm, Markle Street has a beautiful little park with young oak and maple trees, four benches, a play area and bright flower beds on all sides.

Everyone on Markle Street will benefit for years to come from this lovely green haven, all because of your persistence and unwavering belief in the project.

We extend our sincere appreciation for your service. Thank you on behalf of all members.

Sincerely,

William Weeks
Markle Neighborhood Association

CHARITABLE DONORS

Dear Friend,

Some people are extra special, and you are one. As a regular donor to our Shelter Fund, you are someone who really cares when others are suffering and who selflessly goes that extra mile to help out.

I'm writing to thank you from the bottom of my heart and tell you what a huge difference your donations make to our work finding homes for women homeless on the streets. It's such a relief to know you are there. It's only because we can rely on you that we can plan critical programs confidently and push ahead even when demand for our services seems overwhelming.

Quite frankly, you give us the resources to get the job done!

Loyal donors like you have helped us build our downtown facility for emergency shelter and also buy and convert three houses that now permanently house thirty women. With so many turning to us for help, we really need you in our corner. The more generous you can be, the sooner we can help more women put their lives back together.

Please consider an increase in your monthly gift. Your additional contribution would really mean a lot to women who are often homeless through no fault of their own. If you wish to call us, we will be delighted to answer any questions you might have.

You are one of our most precious friends.
Thanks again for caring and helping.

With deepest gratitude,

Greta Joslern
Executive Director

P.S. The extra support you give to the Shelter
Fund, means more help for women who
desperately need a helping hand.
Together, we can give them a safe place
to start over.

NEW CUSTOMER

Dear Ms. Lockwood,

Thank you for making your first purchase at Baboo & Co. We welcome new customers enthusiastically and hope it is the start of a long relationship.

In appreciation, we are enclosing a gift coupon giving a 20% discount on your next purchase. We look forward to serving you well in the future. Please visit us at Baboo & Co. soon.

Yours,

Jacob Hars
Manager

ON BEHALF OF A CHILD

Dear Colin,

Thanks so much for the adorable pink stuffed rabbit you gave Jenny. She loved it the instant she pulled it out of the wrapping and refused to part with it even for a moment.

Right away, she named it Carrots and sleeps with it tucked under one arm. Jenny can hardly wait until your next visit so she can show you the felt hat she is making for Carrots.

You chose exactly the right gift to make a little girl very happy. The whole family would love to see you next Saturday for dinner.

With much affection,

Bette

GRADUATION

Dear Janice,

Congratulations on your graduation. All those nights of hard study really paid off. Now you have a sheepskin in your hand and glowing prospects for the future.

Ever since you used to "organize" the building of snow forts by your friends on the street when you were seven, it was clear you were destined for a career in urban planning. I hear you are starting job interviews next week.

I want to wish you all the best of luck and know you will soon be working your way toward the top of your department in our city.

Wishing you every success,

Aunt Harriet

ENGAGEMENT

Dear Julie and Tom,

Congratulations on becoming engaged. You have always been two of my favorite people. As soon you met, I knew you were perfectly suited. Love was in the air when you both showed up in those matching red jackets, smiling dreamily and holding hands.

With great delight, I watched your early friendship blossom into this wonderful commitment. Your future is bright and I certainly look forward to watching you shine together for many years to come.

Best wishes,

Melanie

WEDDING GIFT

Dear Rachel,

Harry and I just have to tell you how much we adore the magnificent crystal vase you gave us as a wedding present. It looks grand on top of our freshly acquired antique pine bookshelves and is just the right size for the roses we are busy planting in the garden of our new home.

Until the garden blooms, the vase is in constant use holding the armfuls of flowers Harry loves to bring me on his way home from work.

It meant a lot to both of us to have you share our wedding day. Now your vase helps make sure our romance keeps on blooming.

Thanks and much love,

Diane and Harry

DINNER

Dear Liz and Paul,

John and I were so delighted to be included in your dinner party Saturday.

I don't know anyone who can entertain with as much style and imagination as you. The Hawaiian theme was just the ticket to get rid of the winter blahs. Who but you would throw a luau in February!

I'm still humming along with the hula music. I think it's even doing something for my waistline.

Thank you again for such an enjoyable evening.

Warmly yours,

Magda

HOSPITALITY

Dear Tanya,

Thank you so much making my visit to Chicoutimi so memorable.   You invited me into your home and made me feel utterly welcome.

You also took time out from your busy life to show me the highlights of the community and to translate when my lack of language skills almost prevented me from buying that wood carving of a bear and her cub which I now prize so much.

I hope the enclosed snapshots bring back the visit as vividly to you as they do to me.

Much love,

Minnie

HOUSEKEEPER

Dear Mrs. Aleski,

Your help is something this house just can't do without. I want you to know how much we appreciate everything you do for us.

When I come home to a sparkling kitchen and bathroom, beds freshly made up and masses of clean laundry folded and put away, I feel a rush of relief and pleasure.

You and the work you do are very special to our whole household. I can't say enough about how deeply you are valued and hope you feel part of our family too.

Many, many thanks,

Sylvia, Andy, Garth and Jillian

ASSISTANCE

Dear Mr. and Mrs. Wooley,

Last week our car broke down near your home in a driving sleet storm. Since we were on a deserted country road, with no phone, we didn't know what we were going to do. Luckily, you saw our lights and sent your husband out in his truck to see if anything was the matter.

You took our shivering family into your home, made us a delicious hot meal, and called the local mechanic to come and get our car. When our car as fixed, you drove us all to town to pick it up. I honestly don't know what my wife and our two small children would done without your assistance.

It is so heartening to know there are still people willing to help complete strangers. My wife and I want to express our deep and sincere appreciation. We hope we can repay your kindness by helping someone else as much as you helped us.

Very gratefully yours,

Jack and Hilda Miller

BIRTHDAY

Dear Mickey,

Thanks for remembering my birthday. I'm always surprised and gratified when someone outside the family takes note that I've put yet another year under my belt.

Your humorous card gave me a good chuckle. I'll think of it often when I check out my newest laugh lines in the mirror.

Cheers,

Ivan

APOLOGY

Dear Mr. Jackson:

Please accept our sincere apology for the mix-up in reservations last week. I understand how distressing it must have been to drive two hundred miles with your family only to discover no hotel room waited at the end.

Since our staff mislaid your letter, I would like to offer compensation for your inconvenience. Enclosed is a voucher for equivalent accommodation at any hotel in our chain.

We deeply value your good opinion and hope to convince you that this incident is an unfortunate exception to our usual high standard of service.

Yours sincerely,

Arnold Frankener
Manager
Happy Rest Hotels

CONDOLENCE

Dear Joan,

On behalf of the entire family, I would like to offer condolences on the death of your husband, Harry.

Julie and I remember Harry as a man always ready to take time out to help another. One of the reasons we bought our cottage was because of Harry's wise advice. He was a fount of knowledge about the history of the region. Our grandchildren loved the fishing tips he was so willing to share.

Though we only encountered Harry during our summer vacations, he will always be part of our fondest holiday memories and we will miss him very much.

Our hearts go out to you at this difficult time. If there is anything we can do, either now or during the coming summer, please don't hesitate to call.

Warmest regards,

Mac and Julie Semple

Other Phrase Books are Waiting to Help You

The *Fundraiser's Phrase Book* provides thousands of winning phrases designed for the nonprofit professional.

> *"Building blocks you can actually use in your letters, proposals or presentations...an easy escape hatch when you just can't find the right words yourself."*

Canadian Fundraiser

The *Marketing Phrase Book* is for everyone with a product, service or idea to promote.

This amazing thesaurus gives you the language of the marketplace, the language that sells, including *Power Words*, the priceless core vocabulary of selling. Effortlessly write dynamic sales packages, presentations, brochures, advertising, web pages, catalogs, speeches and much more.

> **Words matter. Even the most fluent of tongues gets tied. Which is why the Marketing Phrase Book is such a useful resource."*

Entrepreneur Magazine

These powerful, action-oriented words and phrases help sell millions of dollars worth of products and services every day. Now they're at your fingertips, ready to pull in profits for you. Get ideas! Get inspired! Never struggle for words again!

Check out these endlessly versatile books at:

www.hamilhouse.com

Printed in the United States
209741BV00001B/171/P